EV♡LVE LOVE

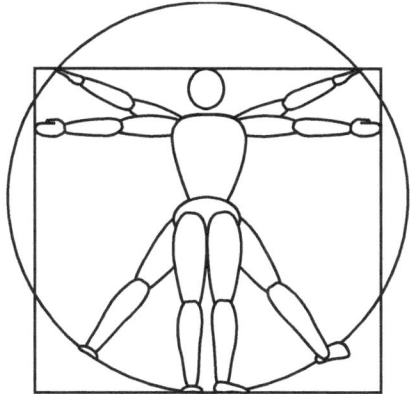

A New Perspective Of Evolution, Love, and Life to
Heal Yourself and the Planet

Written and Illustrated by:

JOHN MYERS CHILDERS

Writers' Branding
(877) 608-6550
www.writersbranding.com
media@writersbranding.com

Acknowledgements

This book is my attempt to understand and explain how my epiphany one morning can help humanity not only over come sexism, racism, bigotry and wars of the modern era, but also how humanity can survive this period of global warming and mass extinction.

I want to acknowledge and thank all of the visionaries and inspired writers who have shaped and added to my understanding of life, love and consciousness including but not limited to; Alan Watts, Piere Teilhard de Chardin, Jean Houston, Barbara Marx Hubbard, Deepak Chopra, Dean Radin, Zach Bush, Marianne Williamson, Michael Bernard Beckwith, Russel Brand, Vandana Shiva, Thich Nhat Hanh and his article on inter-being in Resurgence Magazine,Shunryu Suzuki and Zen Mind, Beginners Mind. Peter Russell and The Global Brain, Marilyn Ferguson and The Aquarian Conspiracy, Fritjof Capra and The Turning Point, Bruce Lipton and The Biology of Belief, Bernardo Ustream and Why Materialism is Baloney, Richard Rosen and The Yoga of Breath, James Nestor and Breath:The New Science of A Lost ArT, Charles Eisenstein and The More Beautiful World Our Hearts Know is Possible, Howard Eisenberg and Dream It To Do It: The Science and The Magic, Satish Kumar and You Are Therefore I Am and Radical Love: From separation to Connection with the Earth, Each Other, and Ourselves, James Lovelock and The Gaia Hypothesis, Jude Currivan and The Cosmic Hologram: information at the Center of Creation and The Story of Gaia, Michael Tabot and The Holographic Universe: A Revolutionary Theory of Reality, Georg Feurstein and The Yoga Tradition, Anodea Judith and The Wheels of Life, Stephen Jay Gould and Of Hens Teeth and Horses Toes, New Dimensions Radio and interviews with David Bohm and many others and finally amazing podcasters on these themes of consciousness, evolution, ecology, quantum physics, love and life such as Commune, Inspired Evolution, Climate Critical, Moment with Marianne Pestana, Future Humans, Conscious Living Network, Buddha at the Gas Pump, Andre Duqum, Rich Roll, Aubrey Marcus, Blu, Science and Nonduality, Wake the Fake Up and more.

I want to especially thank Cindy Hillas for without whose support and love this book would not have been possible.

Table of Contents

MY EPIPHANY

In the fall of 2018, I was active in the elections. I had signs for my city council candidate, mayor, state assembly representative and Congressperson on my front yard. To my immense joy all four of them won. However, after I took the signs down, I felt a lack of direction. Now what?

I thought I would meditate on it. I spent a couple of weeks reflecting, contemplating and meditating on what to do next. Then one morning an epiphany, an image, a vision, a new perspective came to me all at once. I have been a Zen yoga meditator and teacher for decades yet this epiphany was a new revelation to me. It was like a moment of enlightenment and an invitation to a new way of being. I put pen to paper.

EV ♡ LVE

It was not just a word, nor just an image. It was a new and totally different perspective, a paradigm shift in my understanding of reality, evolution, love and life. It has become an insight to complex questions of ontology, the metaphysical nature of our being, and cosmology, the origin and development of the universe. This image thought perspective has captured my imagination and has become the foundation of my cosmology and ontology for a sense of oneness, consciousness, life, self, love and reality.

I painted my epiphany, my image word perspective, over one of my election 2018 signs and stuck it back on my front yard. I painted it again and again adding deeper understandings of this new perspective of evolution, love and life. This epiphany has become an invitation to a new way of imagining, viewing, understanding, and experiencing consciousness, evolution, love, self and society. In short it has become a key to imagine a new cosmology, ontology and philosophy of evolution. It has become a signpost to a cosmology and ontology of oneness, one mind of one heart, of one cosmic inter-being presence and spirit. In other words, I believe that there is one cosmic universal inter-being consciousness which is the ground of all being and existence.

I started imagining, thinking and writing about what it might mean to have a totally different perspective, a 6th Sense of reality, evolution, life, love and society. I started to imagine how to transform the current dominant modern paradigm and cosmology and its materialist perspective of reality. I began to imagine how to manifest a new and different, yet ancient, perspective of evolution and life.

This book is about a cosmology and ontology of oneness, of one cosmic inter-being consciousness responsible for the evolution of everything. It is a call for a global paradigm shift and an evolution of modern values. It is about evolving our connection, coherence and perceptions of each other and our relationship to nature to heal ourselves and the world.

This book is a manual for imagining, transforming, and evolving through physical, spiritual, metaphysical and paranormal practices. It contains the practices, which led to my epiphany, and practices I discovered while writing this book. I invite you to take these practices to heart and take a transformational leap of consciousness into a cosmology of oneness and perceive yourself as a localized cosmic inter-being spirit. In other words, this book is about how humanity can evolve our modern romantic and family understanding of life and love to include a cosmic inter-being love of life, of ourselves, others and the planet. This book is to encourage you to evolve love and become a conscious inter-being and join the tribe of all life on earth. In many ways this book is a continuation of my book, <u>A Yoga Pill For Every Ill: Therapeutic Hatha Yoga</u>, where I concluded the book considering how people could not only heal their physical ills through yoga therapy, but also how they could help heal the ills of the world.

It was February of 2020 when a friend of mine, Angello A. Paparelli, suggested I could write a short hundred-page spiritual book. I thought I would give it a try. COVID-19 arrived in less than a month. At first the pandemic crushed my momentum for writing this book, and then it gave me more time at home to write and reflect on how to evolve my new cosmology of oneness, consciousness and an inter-being sense of self, life, love and society to survive climate change, mass extinction, social injustice, war and ecocide of the modern era. Now that the pandemic is considered endemic I invite you to evolve love, a cosmic love, for yourself, others and the planet.

A NEW PERSPECTIVE OF REALITY, EVOLUTION, LOVE AND LIFE A COSMOLOGY OF ONENESS

I invite you to imagine a new and totally different perspective of reality, an ancient yet quantum perspective of reality, evolution, life and yourself. Imagine that a universal cosmic oneness, one sacred universal cosmic consciousness, is the ultimate source of reality that created everything from atoms to galaxies to life. Imagine that one cosmic fractal holographic field of consciousness, not solid matter, is the origin of the universe, and our ultimate ground of being. Imagine that the galaxies, planets, life and yourself are all expressions of this universal cosmic field of spiritual holographic oneness. That is to say, that at the core of our being, we are all unique localized spiritual aspects of one cosmic inter-being consciousness. We are like localized individual cosmic waves, fractals, or whirlpools in an ever-expanding holographic universe, a cosmic stream of consciousness.

On the surface we appear as individual waves, fractals or whirlpools totally unique and different from each other, yet we are all totally connected and made of the same cosmic inter-being essence.

Now imagine that the impulse of this cosmic consciousness to live and grow is an impulse to expand the universe into greater complexity, biodiversity, connectivity, coherence and consciousness. In other words, the evolution of the universe is not the result of collisions of random bits of matter but rather the expansion of a purposeful intelligent cosmic consciousness. I invite you to consider that the universe is evolving itself into greater complexity through endless cycles of life, death and rebirth. It is not difficult for me to imagine that the evolution of the universe is an intelligent, spiritual, and compassionate phenomena which ultimately is evolving and expressing itself through you and me, and all of life. Let us evolve love, a sacred cosmic love for ourselves, others, and the planet as unique aspects of one cosmic inter-being consciousness. This new and totally different perspective of evolution and reality, this cosmology of consciousness, is a beautiful cosmic oneness, a cosmic love story in which all of life is sacred, connected, interrelated and inter- nested.

Each tree is lovingly inter-nested into a symbiotic relationship with the bacteria and fungi in the soil. Human beings are also lovingly inter-nested into a symbiotic relationship with our gut micro-biome of bacteria and fungi. These recently discovered interdependent inter-nested symbiotic relationships are now referred to by scientist as holobionts. That is to say that scientists have discovered that plants and animals have critical symbiotic relationships with other life forms and no longer can be considered as discrete individual life forms, but rather they need to be considered as complex symbiotic biomes, or holobionts. Now take the leap from considering yourself as a physical interdependent holobiont in a cosmology of materialism to a holographic spiritual inter-being in a cosmology of cosmic oneness. This cosmology of oneness is ultimately an expression of one inter-being cosmic mind spirit manifesting life, us, and all of existence.

However, to include a cosmic sacred inter-being love and connection in the evolution of the universe at this moment in human history will require a change in our perception and understanding of nature, evolution and all of reality. Let us imagine, dream of and perceive that one divine spirit, one meta mind and meta heart, one beautiful cosmic consciousness is expanding the universe and is ultimately the source of everything and everyone. Consider that you and I are part of this and are here to evolve and co-create more complexity, biodiversity, connectivity and coherence through a cosmic inter-being love and connection.

To awaken to and remember this cosmology of consciousness, of one meta mind and heart, of a beautiful cosmic oneness, is to be one with nature, Mother Earth, World Mother, Living Earth, the Greek concept of Gaia or the ancient Inca concept of Panchamama. It is to manifest one cosmic love beyond romantic, self or parental, love to include a cosmic sacred love and connection with the tribe of all life on earth. That is to say, you can see one beautiful universal cosmic inter-being twinkle in everything, and everyone's eyes.

To evolve consciousness for this new and different philosophy of reality and life, for this story of cosmic oneness, at this moment in history will require a paradigm shift, a revolution in values, a sea change, in modern human perception and understanding of reality, the origin of the universe and the nature of being. Making an invisible untouchable space of consciousness, of cosmic oneness, as primary, and visible touchable matter secondary in our thoughts, lives and institutions, turns upside down, inside out and backwards, our conventional modern society, science, medicine and religion. This change of script, this paradigm shift, will conflict and collide with habits, thoughts and beliefs of modern society.

To evolve love and believe in this cosmology of one interdependent and interconnected cosmic inter-being spirit is to awaken our 6th Sense of perception, a metaphysical cosmic love connection and perception, which is beyond our five material senses. It is to imagine, dream and awaken to an ancient quantum story, in which one cosmic mind heart spirit consciousness permeates everything, is primary, while matter is considered secondary in the creation and evolution of the universe and life. In other words, evolution is not the result of separate random bits of matter, but rather it is the result of a purposeful intelligent ever-expanding cosmic mind. Let us awaken to the fact that the universe is more of a great thought or spirit, than it is a great thing or machine.

This ancient quantum perspective of reality, evolution and life causes cognitive dissonance with modern thoughts, beliefs and institutions. Awakening to the belief in the unity and primacy of consciousness, clashes with society's belief in scientific materialism. It is transformational to shift from believing in modern scientific materialism to believing everything is ultimately an expression of a cosmic conscious holographic oneness, which is sacred, and animating us.

To adapt a philosophy, cosmology or ontology of cosmic oneness is to no longer separate physical from spiritual, mind from body, head from heart, humanity from nature, or you from me. Our vibrant spiritual connection to the pervading fundamental impulse of one cosmic consciousness to expand the entire universe through a curious alluring cosmic inter-being spirit is in us, as us. However, there is tremendous cognitive dissidence, fear and doubt about questioning or rebelling against our dominant modern materialist science, culture and institutions, and yet it is difficult to ignore the current dire social, political and environmental crises of the present. Awakening to, and perceiving a cosmology of oneness is not something one can easily understand and experience in the dominant culture, in a material matrix of separation. It will require a change of script, a shift of consciousness and a call for the development of a new sense of perception and understanding, a vibrant sense of perception of evolution, spirit, life, and unity beyond our five material senses.

Imagine yourself as a cosmic inter-being and able to sense and perceive a conscious holographic fractal universe where the essence of the whole field is contained in each bit no matter how small or different. That is to say, bacteria and fungi each have their own bit of DNA and a vibrant bit of cosmic inter-being consciousness in them, no matter how small it might be. Imagine that your gut biome of bacteria, fungi and microorganisms is connected to you and can communicate to you as a 'gut reaction'. Could it be that our gut biome is also like our gut brain, or maybe our Gaia mind? This inter-nested symbiotic connection is a subtle sensibility that is beyond our cosmology of separation. Imagine that one cosmic universal inter-being consciousness, not random bits of matter, is the source of your health and well-being.

LISTEN TO THE SONG OF THE UNIVERSE
THE SONG OF LIFE SINGING IN YOU

The word 'universe' is composed of two Latin words, *'uni'*, meaning one, and *'verse'* meaning song, verse or prayer. In ancient spiritual traditions this one song of the universe is described as an unspoken or silent mantra or song, which is silently uttered with each breath. That is to say all of life, the entire universe, is silently singing the same song as it vibrates, lives and breathes. Imagine that every breath you breathe silently sings out a call of the universe to evolve one beautiful cosmic inter-being spirit in you, and the web of life. Imagine that every breath is an invitation and a call for a beautiful, dynamic and coherent universe.

This uni-verse is an affirmative prayer, song or verse acknowledging and celebrating that we are one. In an ancient yoga unspoken mantra every in-breath silently utters something like "That am I", where 'That" refers to any and all of existence. "That" refers to whatever you are sensing or experiencing at the moment, be it the birds, the sky or the clothes you are wearing. Everything is sacred; everything is part of one holographic inter- being universe, and part of you.

Every out- breath silently utters, "I am That". This silent song of the universe is one of integration and interdependence among all species and all existence. The unspoken song of the universe seeks to end the separation between people and even the separation between species. This universal song prayer challenges the notion that the human species is the most important species on earth.

Listen to the song of the universe singing in you as you breathe. As you exhale it is silently singing out, 'I am That', and as you breathe in it is silently singing, 'That' am I.

Exhale, 'I am That.'

Inhale, 'That am I.'

Exhale, 'I am what thou art.'

Inhale, 'Thou art what I am.'

Exhale, 'We are one.'

Inhale, 'One are we.'

Exhale, 'I am.'

Inhale, 'Am I.'

Cup your hands over your ears

To more easily hear the silent song of the universe.

TE PEOPLE

To help me imagine and visualize myself, and you, as cosmic inter-being spirits humming along and embodying a sacred invisible space of inter-being cosmic consciousness, I have created these figures I call 'Te People', short for terrestrial people, people of earth, people of Gaia, or Gaians.

Te People are stylistically designed to quintessentially represent all people on earth. To the best of my ability, I have stylized Te People to have no specific gender, age, race, or nationality. They represent people like you and me. These drawings attempt to stylistically represent an embodied spiritual human being. I would like to offer the gender-neutral pronouns "te" instead of always having to choose between he or she, and "ter" instead of him or her. These drawings are to help us imagine ourselves as embodying a sacred space of cosmic inter-being oneness.

THE FACE OF ONENESS

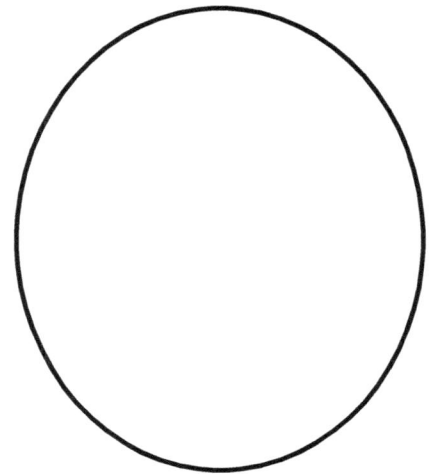

The face of Te People is a face of oneness.

It is the face of one cosmic conscious inter-being animating us.

The face is alert yet calm.

It is like a mysterious and alluring Mona Lisa smiling face.

It is the face we had before we were born.

The Vitruvian

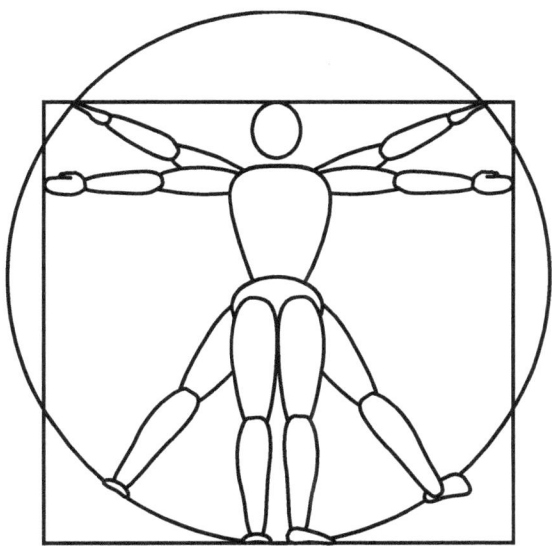

The Vitruvian is a world-renowned drawing created by Leonardo da Vinci representing the quintessential human body. The drawing is based on the correlations of ideal human proportions with the sacred geometry described by the ancient Roman architect Vitruvius. It depicts a human figure in two superimposed positions, with ter arms and legs apart, and simultaneously inscribed in a circle, symbolizing our spiritual nature, and square, symbolizing our physical nature. Leonardo da Vinci believed the workings of the human body to be an analogy for the micro and macro workings of the universe.

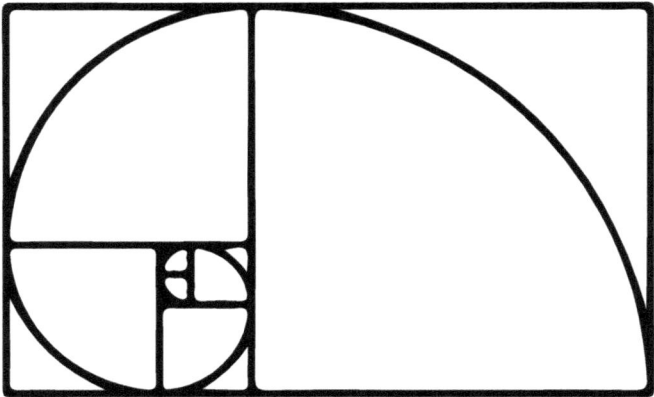

In truth, you and the whole universe are evolving according to a cosmic sacred mathematics and geometry. All of existence is shaped by this sacred original math, a pervading and fundamental cosmic sacred intelligence, mathematics and geometry. For example, the Golden Ratio is the foundation of how the universe, galaxies, pinecones and sunflowers expand and grow. The Golden Ratio is a product of the Fibonacci series and forms the Golden Spiral. The Fibonacci series begins with the numbers 0, 1, 1, 2, 3, 5, 8, 13, 21, 34, 55… This series is produced through the addition beginning with 0+1=1, then 1+1=2, and so on with 1+2=3, 2+3=5, 3+5=8, 5+8=13, etc. The Golden Ratio is the relationship between the numbers of the series. The Golden Ratio is an irrational number that cannot be expressed or written down for it is eternally evolving with the numbers in the Fibonacci series. Phi evolves in the relationship between 8 divided by 5, which is 1.6, and next numbers in the series, 13 divided by 8, which is 1.625. Phi is 1.61803… forever evolving between them. As we continue in the series with 21 divided by 13, which is 1.6153… a number a little less than Phi, yet still closer than before.

Phi is called the most beautiful number in the universe for it is the template onto which all existence evolves. Galaxies, flowers and animals all grow, expand and evolve according to Phi. Petals on flowers appear according to the Fibonacci sequence. Look at your hands. The ratio of the length of the 3 bones in your fingers follows the Golden Ratio.

For example, the tip of your finger could be 3 units long and the next section will be 5 units and the last section of bone is 8 units connecting the finger to the hand. The relative lengths of your fingers could also be expressed in units of 5, 8 and 13 in their attempt to embody the Golden Ratio. The point is that these sacred geometrical relationships are fundamental and found throughout the universe. We, and all of existence, are all connected together in one cosmic Golden Spiral of sacred geometry.

Shiva Nataraja \ The Cosmic Dancer

The Dancing Shiva, Shiva Nataraja or the Cosmic Dancer represents a divine being, which has both masculine and feminine qualities. The figure has broad shoulders like a man, and a narrow waist and wide hips like a woman. Shiva Nataraja, the Cosmic Dancer, is forever dancing out the cosmic impulse of the universe to expand into greater complexity and life. One hand is holding a drum, and the other hand is holding a ball of fire, symbolizing the cycles of creation and destruction, of birth and death and rebirth. Another hand of Shiva points to the raised foot, which symbolizes liberation; while another hand is open and uplifted indicating that we need not fear the cosmic dance of life.

The Cosmic Dancer is the quintessential symbol of the cosmic dance of subatomic matter, life and of mystical spiritual practices of transforming the body into spirit, into an embodied spirituality. Nataraja is dancing on the back of a demon of material fascination who is ignorant of any spiritual nature. The Cosmic Dancer is associated with a transubstantiated body, an adamantine, divine or rainbow body. The Cosmic Dancer connects seemingly contradictory elements of our being such as physical and spiritual, destruction and creation, masculine and feminine, in a giant cosmic dance.

A COSMOLOGY OF ONENESS SERVES AS A FOUNDATION FOR BOTH OUR SPIRITUALITY AND SCIENCE

Imagine that this cosmology of oneness, this philosophy of cosmic unity, of one cosmic inter-being spirit consciousness evolving the universe is a beautiful cosmic love story and can serve as the foundation of all spirituality and science. This fractal holographic cosmology of oneness expanding the universe into greater complexity, connectivity, coherence, consciousness and beauty can serve as a model for both our scientific minds and spiritual hearts. This cosmology of oneness is physical and rational, while being spiritual and irrational. Let us remember that cosmic consciousness is the quintessence of all reality and life.

A cosmology of oneness, of consciousness, of one cosmic mind and heart, of one universal cosmic inter-being spirit animating all life is an ancient indigenous view of life and also a post-modern quantum perspective of the universe. It is a non-binary, a non-dual philosophy of reality and self in which one cosmic mind spirit consciousness is the ground of all existence. In other words, it is not an either-or polarizing philosophy of matter or space, head or heart, you or me, humanity or nature. All of life is ultimately animated by a localized aspect of one cosmic inter-being spirit, which all of life can recognize.

Modern classical Newtonian science still has not found a complete quintessential explanation of consciousness, or a unified theory of reality. Empirical scientists continue to overlook consciousness and love as primary, or even necessary, in the evolution of the universe and life. Nevertheless, many quantum physicists such as David Bohme, a student of Albert Einstein, have suggested that space is an invisible implicate order, a wholeness of infinite connection and potential. This implicate order of space is not an empty vacuum, rather in the words of David Bohm space is full, a 'plenum' of subtle energy, frequency and vibrations. Imagine that this 'implicate order' of the universe is within the quantum space of the atom and the black hole at the center of our galaxy, and is ultimately behind the explicate order, visible touchable matter.

Let us imagine a holographic ecological unified theory of reality where there is a connection and dynamic relationship between the microcosm and the macrocosm, between an organism and its environment, between atoms and galaxies. Let us imagine a unified theory of the universe where there is a connection between physical and spiritual, head and heart, humanity and nature, and you and me. Imagine that the universe is an ever- expanding holographic field of cosmic inter-being intelligence and connection, a cosmic hologram which is the ultimate source behind any phenomenon operating in the universe.

Quantum mechanics, the study of the subatomic world of photons, electrons and quarks, now leads a scientific revolution, which is transforming our separating polarizing conceptions of matter and space, physical and spiritual, body and mind. Quantum theory is creating a scientific revolution that includes consciousness and creates the possibility of merging the polarized concepts of matter and space, self and society, of head and heart into a unified holographic field of cosmic oneness. The famous double-slit experiment rocked the scientific world with a cosmic paradox, when it revealed the wave/particle duality of light, the light behaves *either* like a flowing wave of energy on one hand or like a beam of particles, photons on the other. Light it seems expresses different complementary qualities, wave or particle, depending on how it is observed. Consider that light, an aspect of reality, is affected by you observing it. Imagine and awaken to the fact that light, and ultimately all of reality, could be observed as either wave spiritual or particle physical phenomena.

Quantum theory revolutionizes classical Newtonian physics as it argues that the observer effects the observed, replacing the belief that scientists and people could, passively and objectively, observe electrons, people and nature from a distance. Quantum theory, like ancient spiritual wisdom, considers the whole universe to be connected. As Niles Bohr, quantum physicist, Nobel Laureate put it, "We have to deal with a wholeness that is completely foreign to classical physics." Quantum mechanics has shown how, in this wholeness foreign to classical physics, subatomic particles once connected are forever entangled, even if separated by a vast distance. Imagine the wholeness, a unified holographic field, which connects and unites everything together is an implicate order of cosmic inter-being consciousness. Imagine that this implicate order of cosmic consciousness is the wholeness that is greater than the sum of its parts.

Imagine that an ever-expanding cosmic stream of consciousness is the power and the source of the evolution of everything including you. In this cosmology of oneness everything is spiritual, vibrating, resonating and connected together in a cosmic love story. Scientists have described tiny subatomic particles, quarks, as "allured" to one another.

Water molecules are described as being "attracted" to one another. Consider that plants have feelings and communicate with each other, metals have moods, and rocks have faces. Imagine that the rock we live on, earth, has a face, is alive and has a spirit. The ancient Greeks called this cosmic inter-being earth spirit Gaia, while the ancient Incas called it Pachamama or World Mother. Imagine that all of creation on earth is animated and nurtured by this cosmic earth spirit called Gaia, Pachamama and World Mother. Imagine that your physical constitution is animated and informed by a planetary cosmic inter-being spirit called Gaia, which is animated and informed by the sun of our solar system, which is a child of our milkyway galaxy, which is ultimately a child of our universe.

To imagine and adapt a cosmology of oneness, of one cosmic mind, spirit and love, animating and connecting the entire universe, will require a paradigm shift, an evolutionary leap, from the modern cosmology of materialism and separation. It will require a sea change in humanity's perceptions of reality, self and life. It is a revolution in modern values, thoughts and beliefs to bring the physical and spiritual together, to integrate body and mind, and physiology and psychology. To evolve a cosmology of oneness is to experience and know that a subtle cosmic consciousness occupies all space. It is to know the Ultimate Reality. Everything is sacred: everything is connected. Let us evolve a cosmic love and look into the eyes of each other and all of creation to witness one beautiful cosmic inter-being twinkle.

Albert Einstein said that the most important decision you will make in your life is whether you decide that the universe is a friendly or unfriendly place. It is a question of perception whether you believe and perceive that people and the natural world are basically friendly or unfriendly. It is time to take a leap from fear of an unfriendly universe to co-create with a friendly one. Only by believing and perceiving that the universe and nature are friendly places can we grasp the notion that the ultimate power of the universe is an alluring, attractive and friendly cosmic inter-being spirit, which is behind the evolution of everything.

Let us know and experience this cosmic oneness. Nevertheless, there are no words that can truly describe or even directly speak to this cosmic oneness, this cosmic universal inter-being spirit. However, let us consider that we can resonate with this cosmic inter- being animating us and all of reality. Consider that each cell phone responds to a unique microwave frequency, and as a localized aspect of cosmic consciousness we each have a unique inter-being cosmic microwave frequency or tone.

Let us connect to our unique inter-being cosmic frequency or tone by humming. Humming integrates our body and mind, our heart, gut and head. Humming is a universal language. Humming is a language all life can understand and resonate with. Let us hum, resonate and communicate with each other as global villagers, as members of the tribe of all life on earth. Resonate with one inter-being cosmic vibration of consciousness, hummmm.

Practice connecting, communicating and expressing yourself through humming. Practice humming, agreeably nodding your head up and down, hum – hum. Practice disagreeing humming turning your head side to side, hum – hum. Practice questioning humming, hum? Practice delicious humming, hum-hummm. Practice laughter humming, hum-hum-hum.

A Humming Meditation

Connect to the cosmic hum of the universe. Resonate with the cosmic oneness. Connect and resonate with the hum of our beautiful vibrating living conscious universe and biosphere. While humming, imagine the background hum of the universe, the echo of all creation in you.
Hum along with the universe, your friends and all of life.
Practice for seven breaths.

Hum A Favorite Song.

I feel more confident humming songs than I do singing songs.

In the morning I like to hum the song "Morning Has Broken."

OUR MODERN COSMOLOGY OF MATERIALISM

Our modern cosmology of materialism is a mechanistic and reductionist philosophy based on the notion that the universe, the earth, life and consciousness can be reduced to a sum of separate random physical building blocks of matter, as opposed to a cosmology of oneness where the universe is created from an intelligent and purposeful cosmic inter- being consciousness. Materialism was founded on the belief that matter is solid, inert, lifeless and unconscious. Materialism offers a functional, instrumental and utilitarian perception of people and life. It creates a soulless matrix of separation where material possessions, money, physical objects and private property are more important than aesthetics, relationships, the environment, consciousness or love.

Modern materialism is a reductionist and hierarchical philosophy in which the universe is built up from solid discrete building blocks of matter called atoms. The word atom comes from the Greek *atomos* meaning not able to be cut or divided. The foundation of our modern thought, institutions and culture are based on a dualist and polarized cosmology of random solid matter disconnected by empty space. This separating and polarizing model of reality is an either-or model, a dualist model reality, which separates matter from space, physical from spiritual, body from mind, us from them, humanity from nature, you from me, and it is leading to the destruction of life on the planet.

This binary polarized model creates a matrix of separation, disconnection, competition and hierarchy. The world is structured into polarized thinking of you or me, yes or no, winners or losers, medicine or poison. As this ideology of separation and materialism is applied to living systems and social interactions, the web of life and society become a mechanical sum of discrete separate individual parts with no connection, common purpose, collective or shared identity. That is to say no sense of oneness, fellowship, unity or a sense of interdependence.

YOU AND THE EARTH ARE MORE
THAN MARVELOUS MACHINES

Our modern Newtonian science of materialism might describe your body, your physical constitution, as a marvelous machine, or an elaborate collection of parts and systems that constitute a whole. Describing our bodies, life and the earth as marvelous machines and ultimately as bits of matter has been a corner stone of Western thought. Up until the quantum physics of the 20th century, modern science was based on the notion that the universe was built up from solid matter. Quantum mechanics has shown that atoms are 99.999% quantum vacuum space. That means you are less than 0.001 physical biological matter. Challenged by the presence of the existence of a mysterious quantum space of infinite possibilities, 'quantum foam', modern science and culture typically continues to hold on to two fundamental illusions.

Matter is the illusion of some-thing,

and Space is the illusion of no-thing.

Nevertheless, matter, not quantum foam, is the general term for the substance of which everything and everyone is supposedly made. Scientifically matter has been described as having mass and occupying space. For modern science, matter has been considered an inert solid, while space has been considered an empty nothingness.

Consciousness, thoughts and love were considered products of, or the epiphenomena of, solid inert matter creating a matrix of materialism, in which there is no need of consciousness or love to explain and connect phenomena.

Space has been considered an invisible nothingness, yet now science finds space is full, a 'plentum' of subtle frequencies, vibrations and apparently an incredible amount of untapped potential energy. For hundreds of years science has divided reality and people into mutually exclusive objects and concepts disconnected and separated by an empty space.

The scientific method, the foundation of classical physics and modern science, has made empirical and objective experimental activity paramount. Only what could be measurable and observable with our five material senses in a repeatable experiment was considered valid evidence based science. Matter was measurable, and the invisible world of feelings, thoughts, consciousness, love and beliefs were not. Matter was primary, and our consciousness secondary. Our consciousness has been described by empirical science as being a product of matter, of our brains, our 'gray matter.'

With the rise of manufacturing and industrialization, science started to present our bodies, our physical constitution, and for that matter everything else, as marvelous machines. Plants, animals and the biosphere where considered to be made up of parts and mechanical clock like devices that could be 'fixed' independent of any consciousness, wholeness, feelings or beliefs. Modern science has reduced life, our bodies and even society to a sum of separate parts and systems, and then studies and tries to fix them independently. This reductionist thinking has a subtle and not so subtle implication that the body and society function like machines, and people do not need to be consciously involved in being healed or 'fixed'. This polarized model separates our personal spirit, love and beliefs, from our bodies in healing, work and society.

To have a cosmology and ontology of one cosmic life and consciousness is to identify with the earthly inter-being spirit Gaia, which is evolving and expressing itself as you, others and the web of life on earth. The notion that we can, or will fix our body and physical constitution, or our economy and legal constitution without addressing our beliefs, consciousness or relationships with each other, Gaia and ultimately the universe is completely bogus.

LET US GET OFF OF OUR THRONE OF SEPARATION AND MATERIALISM

In order to get off of our throne of separation we well have to change our physical posture as well as our mental posture, worldview and cosmology of materialism and separation. Our physical posture when sitting or standing generally reflects our mental and psychological posture and thinking.. In other words, our emotional and mental feelings and thoughts directly effect our physical health and vice versa.

It is a paradox that our emotional, mental and spiritual issues

Reside in our physical tissues.

Misaligned physical posture occurs when the head is thrust forward and tilted up so the tip of the nose is above the middle of our ear, the flow of energy is restricted. When the heart is sunken and collapsed, the flow Gaia's love spirit consciousness to our hearts is reduced. To connect our skeletal muscular tissues with our emotional, mental and spiritual issues is to align our spine, our core, our heart and head with Gaia,

When we slouch, while seated or standing, we can often feel deflated, exacerbated or exhausted. When we slouch we feel uninspired. Poor posture makes it difficult to expand the heart cavity and tends to disconnect and separate hearts and heads. Poorly aligned posture disconnects us from our spiritual sense of oneness. A disconnected and misaligned posture reduces the flow of the breath through the body, and the ability to get grounded and aligned to connect, and tune into Gaia.

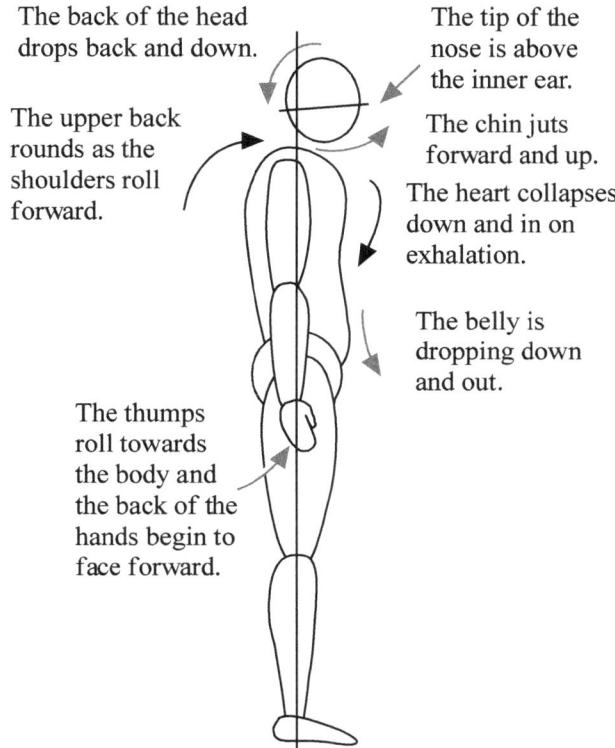

The back of the head drops back and down.

The tip of the nose is above the inner ear.

The upper back rounds as the shoulders roll forward.

The chin juts forward and up.

The heart collapses down and in on exhalation.

The belly is dropping down and out.

The thumps roll towards the body and the back of the hands begin to face forward.

You can get grounded and tune into a cosmology of oneness and Gaia's love and wisdom in any moment and in any posture. However, good posture will make it easier. Good sitting postures are considered ideal for breathing practices, meditation and experiencing a sense of oneness. The secret to taking a seat for meditation and getting grounded is to get off your throne of separation. To get off of your throne of separation is both a psychological and physiological activity. It is to take a seat and be present not sitting back into feelings of pride or pity. Consider perching on your seat, calm and alert without tension. Take a seat so that you can be present not reliving memories or projecting into the future. Take a seat so that you can connect your heart and head, body and mind, align the spine and tune into the vortex field of inter-being consciousness with Gaia. Take a seat and experience a deep connection to Gaia.

Chairs symbolize thrones of status, authority and power in modern society. We say things like, 'to have a seat at the table' or 'to sit at the head of the table.' To be in a person with the most power is the 'chairperson'. Additionally, a sense of royalty and separation abounds in the common expression, a man's home is his castle. Therefore, people like to feel like a king or a queen sitting back on a throne on their porch, or in their living room.

The thought that humanity is separate from nature allows people to feel like they can sit on a chair or a throne separate from the earth, society and the web of life.

Begin by leveling the pelvis. Anchor the pelvis to the earth through your sitz bones, the thick prominences of the pelvis that support weight while sitting. The knees should be level with or below the hips, otherwise you might lose a level pelvis. Anchor your sitz bones into your seat, create a plumb line through the middle ear, shoulder and hip, and get connected to the gravitational field of the earth. Allow the lower abdomen to move with the breath and lift the heart as you inhale. Leaning back on a sofa or chair will round the back so that the spine no longer aligns with the gravitational field of the earth and the abdomen is no longer free to move with the breath, and therefore diminishing any spiritual connection. Being barefoot will help you be even more grounded and connected with Gaia.

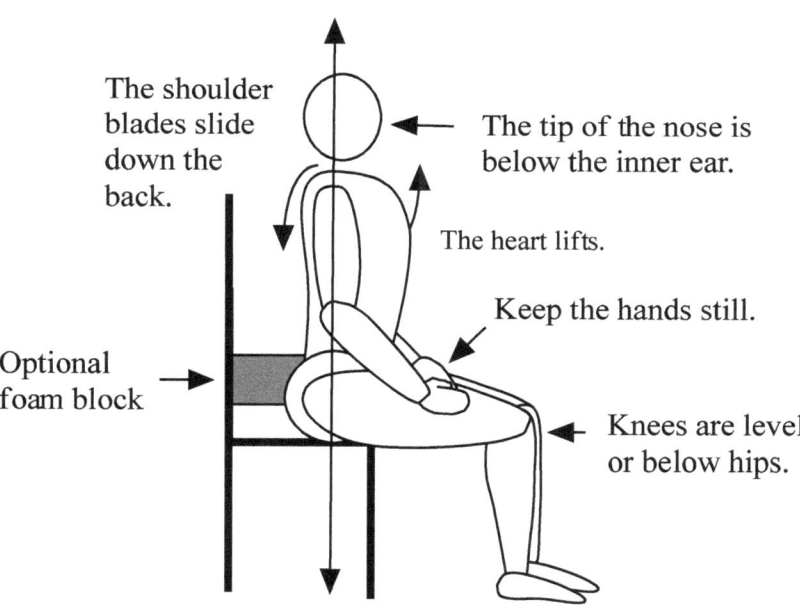

The shoulder blades slide down the back.

The tip of the nose is below the inner ear.

The heart lifts.

Keep the hands still.

Optional foam block

Knees are level or below hips.

To help support a level pelvis, place a foam block, firm cushion or a rolled-up yoga mat between the back of the chair and the sacrum. This is not support for the low back or the upper back. This is support for the sacrum to help level the pelvis.

When sitting on the floor, raise the pelvis by sitting on a cushion, block or folded blankets so the knees are below the pelvis and the natural curve of the low back can be maintained. Maintain a dynamic tension between left and right, lifted and rooted, and front and back.

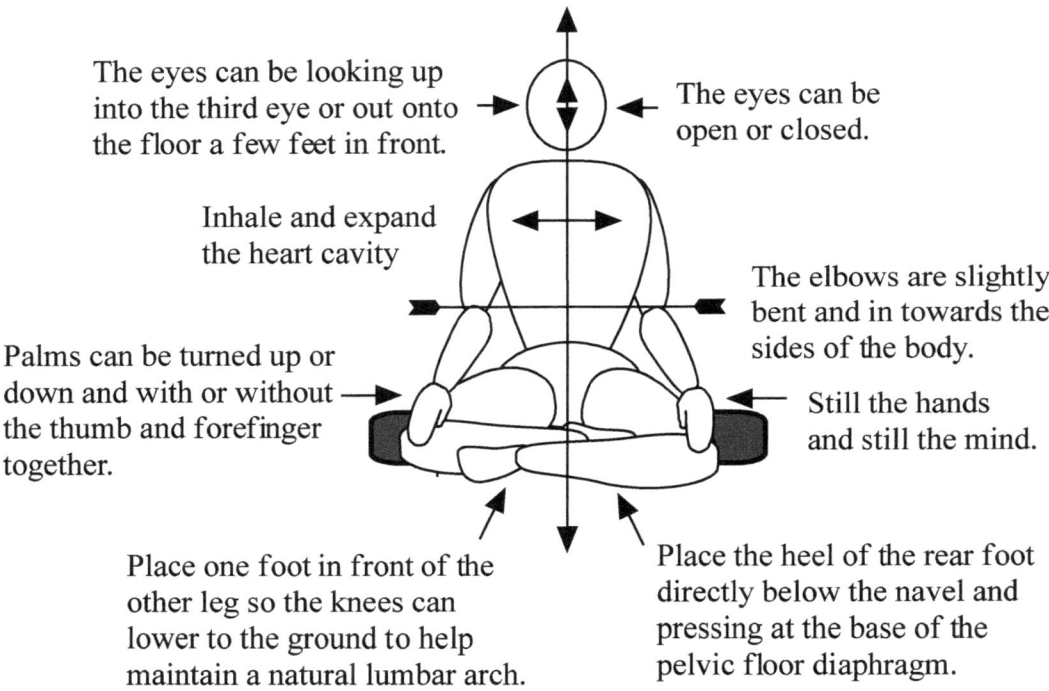

The eyes can be looking up into the third eye or out onto the floor a few feet in front.

The eyes can be open or closed.

Inhale and expand the heart cavity

The elbows are slightly bent and in towards the sides of the body.

Palms can be turned up or down and with or without the thumb and forefinger together.

Still the hands and still the mind.

Place one foot in front of the other leg so the knees can lower to the ground to help maintain a natural lumbar arch.

Place the heel of the rear foot directly below the navel and pressing at the base of the pelvic floor diaphragm.

Pain and anxiety are like ungrounded static energy not moving through the body.

Exhale and ground any static energy, pain or anxiety.

Inhale and liberate any tension that obstructs the flow of your energy.

DEATH

In our modern cosmology of materialism, your soulless body is not woven into the web of life and the cosmic cycle of birth, death and rebirth. Therefore, if you do not consider yourself as a spiritual being, an expression of an evolving inter-being cosmic consciousness, the death of your physical form is equal to annihilation, kaput, the end. This leads to an unnatural denial, fear and desire to conquer death, thus modern medical treatment is supposed to 'save peoples lives' and typically considers a patient's death as a defeat. Nevertheless, the truth is a doctor cannot save anyone's life. We are all going to biologically die, so it would be wise to acknowledge the stages of life and prepare for our physical death and our spiritual transformation. Let us imagine our death as a beautiful inter-being spiritual evolution and transformation into the next phase of our inter-being existence, not our definitive end.

Our sense of self, our sense of me, in a cosmology of materialism is separate, and in competition with the rest of the web of life. This creates a sense of otherness, of 'not me', where it is ok to kill what is 'not me'. The net result is a modern society, science and culture, which are based on a death dealing philosophy for both thriving and surviving. We have mouthwash to kill germs, antibiotics to kill bacteria, pesticides to kill bugs and wars to kill our enemies. To be successful in a modern business deal is described as 'to make a killing.' As a result, modern society has created a 'death cult' culture where killing is the answer, the go-to solution for our challenges and competition. Furthermore, our materialistic culture leads people to be obsessed with obtaining physical objects and property in an attempt to conquer death. As the modern saying goes, "He who dies with the most toys wins."

However, you can imagine that your physical death will return your vortex of consciousness, your inter-being spirit, back to an ever-expanding stream of cosmic oneness, unconditional love and acceptance. Imagine that our physical death is not something to fear. Imagine that your consciousness, your soul, your cosmic inter-being spirit will continue to evolve through cycles of reincarnation. As a localized aspect of cosmic consciousness or as a whirlpool of consciousness, you will upon your physical death, simply release, and join with the stream of consciousness; or visualize a wave of consciousness that appears and then disappears on the surface of an ever expanding and evolving ocean of cosmic consciousness. Imagine that your spirit, your cosmic inter-being consciousness, is immortal, and that the frequency, the vibration, the hum that is you, will elegantly meld into the symphony of cosmic oneness.

Let us be motivated by an eternal love of life, rather than a temporal fear of death. Let us, as inter-being Gaians, as global villagers, consider the physical impact of our lives will have on the quality and sustainability of the lives of seven generations yet to come. Instead of considering death as your definitive end, consider that your physical death returns your body to Gaia and your consciousness to a cosmic evolving stream of consciousness, love and light.

COLONIALISM

In Europe the modern era began with the combination of the Black Death, the heavy plough, the rise of scientific materialism, mercantile capitalism and colonialism. The modern era marked the end of medieval superstitions, metaphysics and mysticism, and the growth of scientific materialism. However, for much of the rest of the world the modern era meant colonization, domination, genocide and extraction.

The modern era linked scientific progress to human progress. Scientific progress could be defined as humanity's ability to understand, control and dominate nature for its own needs, ends and benefits. The very notion of technological progress, like the plow, pesticides, dams or herbicides, has implied ever-greater control, exploitation and domination over the soil and Mother Earth. Western European scientific progress combined with ethnocentric Christianity led to the domination and control over non- European people with guns and steel resulting in colonialism, genocide and slavery.

Early European concepts of Christianity believed that people who were not Christians were mystics, infidels or pagans, in other words, savages. 15th century papal bulls considered any non-Christians as barbarians, savages and less than human, and therefore could be captured, enslaved or killed. The notion that someone could know God and have a spiritual life with nature, without going through the hierarchy of Christianity were considered heretics, barbarians and savages. Western European Christian duelist cosmology of materialism separated the spiritual and physical, heaven and earth, and humanity from nature creating a hierarchical soulless matrix of life here on earth. In Europe hundreds of thousands of women midwives and herbalists were put to death as witches. Christianity combined with the goals of material progress has led to colonization, genocide and exploitation of all non-European Christian peoples and lands. A cosmology of materialism mixed with Christianity has now led to a Western European colonization and conquest of the globe.

The moment has arrived for modern science and humanity's world's monotheistic religions to realize that their duelist cosmology of materialism, which separates heaven from earth, spiritual from physical, and humanity from nature is resulting in sexism, bigotry, war and the destruction of the biosphere. Let us wake up to the primacy of consciousness and the interdependence of all life on earth. We are separate yet inseparable from each other and the web of life. We are each connected to the depths and source of an evolving and expanding conscious universe.

CAPITALISM

A cosmology of materialism with its matrix of separation creates hierarchical structures. These hierarchical structures rank reality into categories of importance or worth creating systems of caste, class, sex, race and exploitation. Humanity has been considered more important than nature, men more important than women, and those who have private property and status are more important than those who do not have them.

Furthermore, a cosmology of materialism leads to material objects, property and money, as the primary forms of identification and connection between people, while friendship, the biosphere and consciousness are secondary in importance. In our modern cosmology of materialism, the script reads, "Don't take it personally, its just business." That is to say, what is primary and most important in modern society is the world of business, profit and money, and secondary in importance are the invisible personal relationships of family, friends, community and nature. Profits are internalized by capitalists while the global and local destruction of their businesses to environments and ecosystems are considered as externalities and everyone absorbs the costs.

This soulless matrix of materialism is the foundation of modern capitalism and has created a trust and a belief in a system of money and property to define and connect us.

Historically money has been described as a medium of exchange, but upon closer examination money is more like a medium of competition in a matrix of separation, as workers compete for paychecks, as producers compete with prices, as corporations compete for sales of natural resources and so on. Money is a medium of competition in a capitalist society. Money is used to keep score of who is winning or losing in society. In the United States the GDP, gross domestic product, the monetary value of goods and services produced in a certain period, is the most commonly used source to keeps score and judge weather our capitalist society is failing or succeeding.

The trust and belief in materialism, money and a "free market" capitalist economy to guide us is like a modern-day religion, a 'capitalist money-theism'. This 'money-theism' holds the fervent belief that money and the ownership of private property, are good things, and that they can make us happy and safe. Capitalist money-theism grew throughout the 20th century in America. In1956 the United States put the words "In God We Trust" on the dollar bill, replacing the original motto of the United States, "E pluribus unum", Latin for "Out Of Many, One."

The goals, hopes and dreams of a person believing in capitalist money-theism are to own money and property. Modern Christian capitalists have created a prosperity theology and gospel, which believe and preach that money; wealth and prosperity are the will of God. In other words, if you are wealthy in this life, it is the will of God, and you must be a good God loving person. Of course, the opposite is true, if you are poor or not wealthy it is also the will of God and you must be lazy, flawed or at least not a good Christian.

Our traditional use and concepts of money have morphed over time. Today's money is no longer related to silver coins or the gold standard. Modern capitalist money is now 'fiat' money, digital paper money created at will by the state through Central banks and is distributed as debt bearing wealth. This 'fiat' money' is not tied to any real wealth in the world. Money is now manipulated at will by governments and corporations with debt, government bailouts and financial instruments such as credit cards, hedge funds and the IMF - International Monetary Fund. Modern monetary wealth is completely disassociated from the only true sources of wealth, the health and well being of people, animals, plants, air, water and soil.

The matrix of materialism and separation has created a capitalist society of skin- encapsulated egos, narcissists and authoritarian figures. At the same time, it has minimized, corrupted and distorted human social relationships, community and democracy. Money theism distorts the growth of human beings by rewarding them when they are competitive, greedy and distrustful of other human beings. Capitalist money theism is like a cancer in the body of humanity as it disconnects us from any sense of a shared commonwealth or health. It is time for everyone to share in society's technological developments, infrastructure, healthcare and achievements. Maybe it is time to cancel the crushing debt of both individuals and countries currently struggling with massive debt.

Maybe it is a good idea to consider sharing and redistributing the accumulated wealth of society through a universal basic income as a partial solution for the loss of jobs due to automation and to the massive wealth inequality created by modern global capitalism.

In Tolkien's classic trilogy <u>Lord of the Rings</u> the 'ring of power', the 'one ring' is the one ring to rule all other rings of power, and according to the novel, "in the darkness bind them." Money-theism is the "one ring", the "ring of power" in the story of the modern era. The one ring to rule them all in the modern era is money and private property, or in another word, capital. Furthermore, like in the novel, the ring of power, like modern day money and private property, are things that most people believe that they can hold and wield for good. Nevertheless, the ring of power must be destroyed in the novel because even though people thought that it could be used for good, it was inherently evil. This is because the ring was forged by the Dark Lord of Mordor, and ultimately will only serve him. Money theism was forged by the Dark Lord of the soulless matrix of materialism and separation and will only serve to separate people resulting in systems of caste, race and country leading to competition, poverty and war. In the story the ring of power must be destroyed if Middle Earth is to be saved. The modern era ring of power, money complete with materialism, private property and capitalism, must be destroyed for humanity to break free from disconnected and destructive relationships between each other and the web of life.

A fellowship of all the peoples from Middle Earth was required in Tolkien's trilogy to go on the quest to destroy the ring of power. Likewise in the modern era, it will require a fellowship of all the peoples of earth to go on the quest to destroy the modern ring of power, the power of money, private property and global finance capitalism. And like the trilogy, it will probably take the modern era three novels to complete its quest to destroy the ring of power.

Give up the love of power, for the power of love.

Let us give up the modern ring of power, the power of money, the power over others and nature, for the power and presence of one cosmic inter-being consciousness, connection and love, the true source of your authentic power. You were born with an authentic power to imagine, visualize, resonate and co-create with an infinite cosmic love and intelligence. Let us rebel against our skin-encapsulated ego's desire to be a billionaire and live like a king on a throne, and revel in being a sovereign inter-being global villager whose wealth and well being are source in the health and well-being of the biosphere and the family of humanity.

CLEAR YOUR SPIRIT, MIND AND BODY

Clear your mind, body and nose, of the barbarity, genocide and slavery of colonialism. Free your mind of the ills of materialism, capitalist money theism and fear of death. Blow them out your nose.

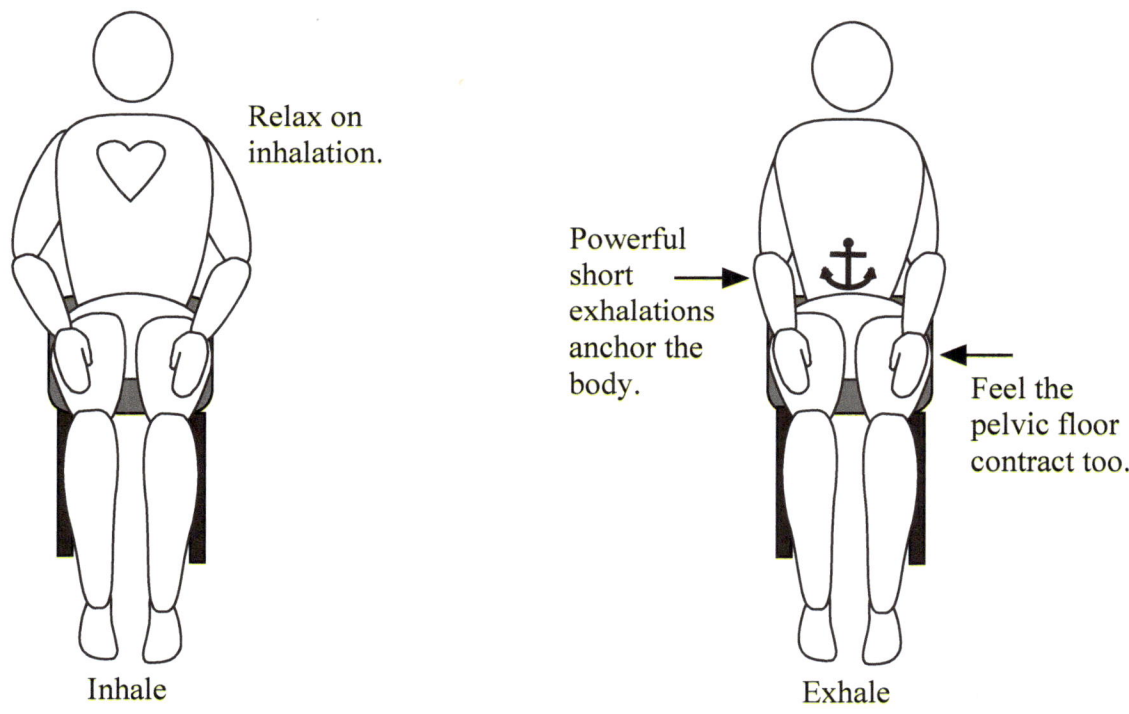

Relax on inhalation.

Inhale

Powerful short exhalations anchor the body.

Feel the pelvic floor contract too.

Exhale

Focus on creating short, sharp and powerful exhalations through your nose..

Exhale sharply and forcefully contracting the rib cage and abdomen down and in, and then simply allow the inhalation in. Repeat 10 times. Pause, move into the stillness and a sense of oneness.

ESPIRITU

The prevailing modern belief that everything can be explained by a cosmology of scientific materialism compels us to think that only what can be scientifically measured can be true and therefore meaningful to us. Thus, for centuries modern science has generally omitted the value and role our consciousness, beliefs, feelings and relationships have on our life and healing. As a result, modern science downplays and ignores the placebo effect, the effect of psychology on physiology, of beliefs on our physical and chemical body, as an unimportant anomaly, when in reality it is amazing proof of the primacy of consciousness in our health and well-being. Let us remember that our invisible beliefs can have an effect on our body's biochemistry as great as any pharmaceutical pill.

To imagine, adapt and believe in a cosmology of consciousness is to perceive that each human being has a unique inter-being cosmic spirit, frequency or vibration, a unique cosmic hum if you will. Let us consider ourselves as localized aspects of one cosmic dance, as whirlpools in a cosmic stream of consciousness, as expressions of one cosmic spirit inter-being evolving into greater complexity, biodiversity and interdependence.

Human beings are more than skin-encapsulated egos whose sole purpose is to maximize self-interest, self-gratification and procreation. The philosophy of a separated self is exemplified by the modern expression, "If everyone took care of himself, or herself, everything would get taken care of." This is a disconnected, fragmented and ultimately a dog-eat-dog philosophy of materialism. Modern materialistic society divides, disconnects and reduces people into separate distinct individuals, as if we were solid atoms separated by empty space.

You are more of a spiritual being having a physical experience, Than a physical being, having a spiritual experience.

In Latin the term espiritu literally meant both spirit and breath. To become conscious of your breath is an intimate and direct path to connecting to your spirit. Our breath unites our material physical form with our formless thoughts, feelings and spirit. The breath affects both our physiology and psychology. Our breath responds to changes in our emotions and thoughts, as well as changes in our levels of physical activity. Our invisible spirit, feelings, thoughts and intentions drive and ride on the wave of the breath throughout our bodies. Still, many people are unconscious of how they breathe, and often claim that they do not know how to breathe, which indicates that they do not connect to their spirits as they breathe.

Basically, we have an in-breath and an out-breath, with a pause after the in-breath and a pause after the out-breath. All together they equal one complete breath, and could be perceived as one complete spiritual connection, a connection between your localized individual inter-being spirit and the universal planetary inter-being spirit Gaia, as you inhale and exhale.

Healthy breathing begins with breathing in through your nose. The nose, with its intricate design, is the optimal choice for breathing during both inhalation and exhalation, during both rest and daily activity. Breathing in through the nose filters, warms, moistens and conditions the air for the lungs. Inhaling through the nose calms and soothes the body and mind, while inhaling through the mouth offers none of the above benefits. Furthermore, the olfactory sensors in the nose stimulate the mind creating even greater consciousness associated with our instincts and intuition. Conscious rhythmic breathing through your nose is a great way to create conscious spiritual connections. Practice consciously breathing in and out through your nose for physical, emotional, mental and spiritual health and well-being.

Inhaling through your mouth stresses your lungs and nervous system and compromises your spiritual connection to the cosmic oneness. Inhaling through the mouth adds to feelings of nervousness, anxiety, stress and fear. Mouth breathing creates dis-ease in our body, mind and spirit. Unconscious continuous mouth breathing during daily activities like walking or doing the dishes indicates a physical, emotional, mental stress or illness as well as a weakened spiritual connection.

To help you be more connected and conscious of breathing through your nose place a finger alongside your nose and close one nostril. Practice breathing in and out through one nostril. Breathing through one nostril will slow your rate of respiration. It will give you more time to notice and experience the inhalation and the pause stillness space between inhaling and exhaling and experience a spiritual connection there. Become aware of the pause in the breath. Tune in to the quality and quantity of your breath and spirit. Now change sides and cover the other nostril and practice conscious breathing through one nostril again. Finally consciously breathe through both nostrils.

Conscious breathing is experienced from the soles of our feet to the top of our heads. The breath does not only organize the exchange of oxygen atoms. Breathing influences the quantity and quality of the flow of blood, lymph and nervous energy throughout the body and mind. It energizes the body's subtle vortex field of energy from head to toe. Conscious rhythmic breathing is our single best medicine for radiant physical, emotional, mental and spiritual well-being.

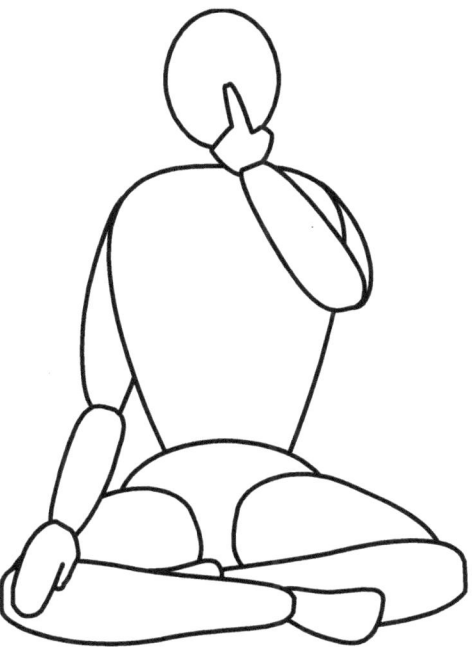

Consciously breathe through your nose and Awaken to a cosmology of oneness, to one cosmic inter-being spirit, love and connection.

In several shamanic traditions around the world the gesture of placing an index finger to the side of the nose is an indication of the journey to the invisible world of spirits. In the famous story, "The Night Before Christmas", the shamanic reindeer herder, super Shaman Santa Claus, places his finger to the side of his nose, and up the chimney he goes on his cosmic journey around the world. I like to think of placing one finger alongside of the nose as an indication, acknowledgment and salutation to the journey of the Gaian global villager, Cosmic Dancer or spiritual seeker of today to evolve love and inter-being consciousness around the world.

EV⊙LVE

EVOLVE LOVE FOR A NON-DUAL PERSPECTIVE OF LIFE

This image can help us visualize the non-dual nature of life and a cosmology of oneness. Life is about balancing the polarities, qualities and hilarities of yin and yang, such as cold and hot, feminine and masculine, east and west, and moonlight and sunlight. Yin and yang are two aspects of one undifferentiated whole, woven together to create one holographic field or as David Bohm would say one implicate order. Yin and Yang are two aspects of a cosmic oneness, like inhaling and exhaling are two aspects of one breath. To be a Cosmic Dancer is to dance between the polarities and hilarities of the dynamic relationships between yin and yang, feminine and masculine, night and day, or lifted and grounded. Simply put non-dual means, not two. In other words, in a non-dual philosophy and cosmology things are not separated into two totally distinct things like black and white or cold and hot. Attune to the cosmic oneness and celebrate and dance with a beautiful rainbow spectrum of reality, life and self.

The breath expresses many dynamic polarities like expanding and contracting, lifted and grounded, feeling and willing, and liberating and manifesting aspects of us. The yin and the yang symbol can help us visualize the breath as one whole breath that oscillates smoothly and rhythmically. Notice that there is a small circle, an element, of yang in the field of yin, and a small circle, an element, of yin in the field of yang. This creates a curious and beautiful paradoxical tension between the two. That is to say, there is an element of being lifted with yin energy while still being grounded with yang energy, and vice versa.

The breath also expresses dynamic emotional, mental and psychological relationships such as feeling and willing, and liberating and manifesting aspects of us. Visualize that the front of the body contains the feeling and liberating aspects of our being, and is connected to our yin inhalations, while the back of our body contains the willing and manifesting aspects of our being which are connected to and open with our yang exhalations.

Our current modern society and culture are totally unbalanced in terms of the qualities of yin and yang. Modern culture has exalted the qualities of the yang masculine, while diminishing the qualities of the yin feminine. In a fundamental way our modern culture is too yang and disconnected from the feminine yin. Let us be more mindful and conscious of our yin feminine breath.

BE MINDFUL TO OPEN, ACTIVATE AND
EXPAND THE FRONT OF YOUR BODY,
THE YIN FEMININE SIDE OF YOUR BODY,
AS YOU INHALE

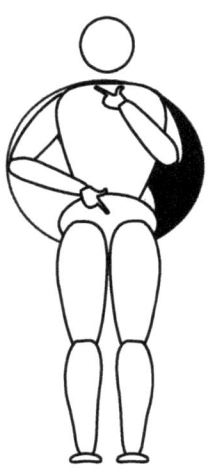

To help you open the front of your body as you inhale, place the forefinger and thumb of one hand on your chest just below the collarbones. Imagine that you could inhale to nostrils below the collarbones. Place the thumb of the other hand in your navel and the fingertips on your pubic bone. Imagine that you could exhale out of your navel.

Now inhale to the imaginary nostrils below your collarbones. Lift and expand your chest and open the front of your body. Feel the lower abdomen and solar plexus expanding and lifting the heart as you inhale. Pause. Hold the front of the body lifted and open with your thumb and forefinger below your collarbones as you exhale out of your navel. Feel a dynamic tension and balance between being lifted and grounded, between inhaling and exhaling.

Repeat 7 times.

LIBERATE ANY TOXIC THOUGHTS OR EMOTIONS

Lie down and place a foam block or stack of folded blankets under the pelvis. Inhale and open the feminine front of the body.
Inhale, expand your solar plexus, and let it lift and expand your heart and liberate any feelings of sadness, shame, grief, guilt or fear.
Inhale and liberate your skin-encapsulated ego. Inhale and liberate yourself from materialism.

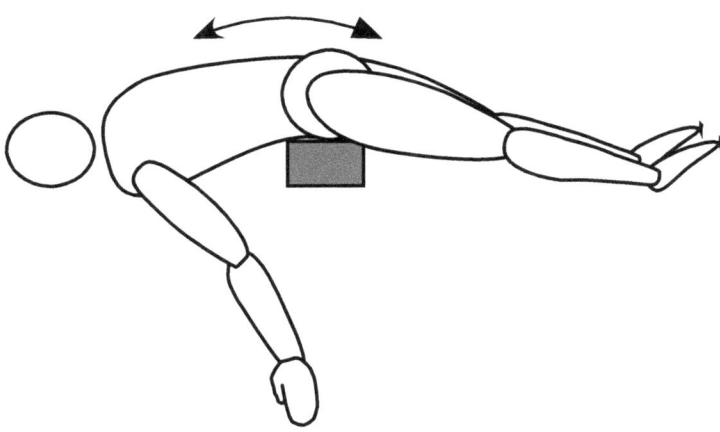

Consider that when people feel stressed, exasperated, exhausted or deflated, they often feel the need to suck the breath in through their mouths to power up. Remember that the weight of 5 miles of atmosphere above us rushes into our lungs as we create a space in the body and lungs for the breath to rush in. Breathing is basically about actively expanding, inviting and welcoming the breath in while inhaling, pausing and connecting to the infinite spirit, and relaxing while exhaling into a pause. Nevertheless, people often habitually suck the inhalation or simply unconsciously breathe in with their mouths open. Remember that the nose knows how to breathe.

To adopt a non-dual cosmology of consciousness, of one head and heart is to connect issues and systems such as inhaling and exhaling, the feminine and the masculine, and the right and left hemispheres of our brains. On a very deep level humanity needs to connect and integrate the qualities of our left and right hemispheres of our brain, of how we perceive, process and understand self and reality. The left hemisphere is the rational reductionist side of our brains, which is grounded in numbers and letters, while the right hemisphere has the intuitive holistic side of our consciousness grounded in image and music

For thousands of years humanity has witnessed the growth, development and dependence on written numbers and letters to construct and explain society and reality. It is interesting to note that the left hemisphere controls are right hand and are right hemisphere controls our left hand, as modern society is so right-handed. Doorknobs, handles and tools are typically designed for the right hand.

It's time to shift and balance modern society and culture from primarily a right- handed left-brain view of reality, the rational reductionist perception expressed through numbers and letters, with the left-handed right brain, a trans-rational understanding of reality, a holistic integrated perspective best understood through image and sound. Let us stop always resorting to numbers to score and evaluate the health, success or failures of institutions and people. Let us integrate the right and left hemispheres of our brain, our understanding of both images and letters, to evolve a new perspective of evolution, life, self and society. To embody spirituality is to create a non-dual holistic connection between the left and right hemispheres of our brain, to connect letters and images, masculine and feminine, self and society, humanity and Gaia, and normal and paranormal aspects of our being. Let us integrate the images of the right brain with the words of the left-brain for a new non-dual perspective of reality, evolution, life, self and society.

Soften your forehead and connect the left and right hemispheres of your brain as you inhale.

Keep your forehead soft as you exhale. Evolve love and open a sense of unity and oneness in your brain as you breathe. Repeat seven times.

FROM A ME SOCIETY TO A WE-ME SOCIETY

Human beings are social animals by nature. Nevertheless, we are all taught in school and society to be a competitive, independent and separate individual, who primarily needs, wants and seeks individual recognition, gratification and achievement before seeking and valuing social relationships, love and nature. Our modern capitalist societies generally define what it means to be an adult as only one's ability to be able to economically, emotionally and mentally support themselves. This leads to a "Me first philosophy, " a "dog-eat-dog" philosophy. This is opposed to a philosophy of interdependence, community and sense of common purpose. Our separate ego sense of self wants to feel independent and able to persevere against all odds. Our ego narcissistic self wants to feel like a king in society, not an interdependent member of society.

Modern capitalism focuses on the needs and wants of a skin-encapsulated ego as it isolates and separates people with separate school desks, paychecks and identity-politics. As a result, people typically are only interested in taking care of themselves and the people they identify with. The image of our modern family is generally restricted to a small circle of blood relatives and friends. Let us evolve and expand our circle of compassion and consciousness to include all of humanity and the web of life.

It is time to shift, from focusing on the liberty and morality of individual personal egos of a "Me Society" to include more socially integrated needs and morality of the whole society and biosphere, a "WE Society". It is a paradigm shift in our modern thought to perceive separate individuals, and their families, as members of one family sharing a common sense of purpose on earth. What we are, who we are, and where we come from Is a shared story of one family of humanity, of one people and of one planet. It is a political ideology which has been summed up in the slogan, "Not Me, Us."

Our ME Society of rugged individualism is based on meritocracy, the notion that people should be rewarded in society based on their merit. However, modern capitalist meritocracy is based on the assumption that there is equal opportunity for all individuals regardless of historical, institutional and structural inequity, sexism and bigotry. Our capitalist meritocracy mantra says that, if you study and work hard you will get ahead.

However, it also implies that if you are poor or not ahead, it is your fault, and you must be lazy, stupid or flawed in some way, and not because of some inherent injustice in the capitalist system of systemic wealth inequality, racism, sexism or xenophobia. Our modern, dog-eat-dog predatory capitalism produces feelings of competition, separation and fear of other people, as if other peoples' pain and struggles, or love and happiness, did not affect us personally. Instead of trying to pull yourself up by your own bootstraps by taking advantage of others or nature, awaken to the truth that we are all connected and need to work and play together to lift ourselves and humanity.

We are all fluid inter-being processes embodied in the web of life. It is amazing to consider that the atoms, which comprise your body, are not your atoms. Humans are constantly exchanging atoms back and forth with each other and the web of life. Every day we are exchanging atoms with nature as we eat, drink and breathe. Every week you exchange a forearm's worth of atoms with the web of life. Within two years every atom, in every cell of your body, is replaced. Every breath you take has trillions of atoms in it. To evolve a love for a cosmology of oneness is to shift from a separate isolated sense of 'ME', to an interconnected and inter-being sense of "WE-ME".

Expand your consciousness and visualize that the words, and concepts of, WE and ME are two sides of the same coin, two sides of humanity. Visualize how the word WE, is the word ME, physically and psychologically, turned upside down. Society needs both a sense of WE and ME. Let us evolve love for a sense oneness and co-create coherence between a sense of ME and WE, between personal needs and morality, and social needs and morality.

Let us, let humanity, take the leap from separation to unification, integration and coherence between a sense of ME and WE, personal needs and community needs, private wealth and public health. A WE-ME Society would be a shift in our consciousness as to what is most important and primary to you, society, and the family of humanity and ultimately the web of life.

It is a paradox that you have to live, heal and grow by yourself,

And yet you cannot do it alone.

Everyone needs help getting out of the womb, into the grave, and someone to lean on along the way. Rebel against a solid separate ego sense of 'ME'. Rebel against the soulless matrix of separation and materialism. Revel in Gaia and a cosmology of oneness, of one inter-being an inter-nested web of life. Co-create connectivity, coherence, consciousness, love and light in yourself and others, and allow them to witness and co- create it in you. Remember, your life is inseparable from others and the biosphere. In a fundamental symbiotic way, caring for others and nature is ultimately taking care of us.

THE SPACE WHICH CONNECTS US

To connect and resonate with the minds and hearts of others and the tribe of all life on earth is to connect and embody the pause, the stillness, the space in the breath, a space that connects we and me, Gaia and the family of humanity.

Visualize the pause, the stillness, the space, at the top of the inhalation and then again at the bottom of the exhalation. Or visualize a pendulum swinging back and forth into and out of a pause, a moment of stillness and a space of dynamic oneness. Feel and experience this pause, stillness, and cosmic space. This cosmic space that is you is the final frontier for the explorers, Cosmic Dancers and spiritual seekers of today, for the final frontier is to occupy and embody a space of inter-being oneness. Imagine this totally different consciousness of inter-being and don't freak out over how a WE-ME Society is going to take care of you and others when it is difficult for so many of us to personally make a living and take care of ourselves in our ME society.

Remember, this paradigm shift, this sea change of consciousness, to a WE-ME society is not about losing something, or having more of something that we have already had in our modern materialistic ME society. It is about having something different, a different perspective, consciousness and set of values for what it might mean to live and work, as a global villager in a space of inter-being oneness with a common purpose to co-create and regenerate life, together in a WE-ME society, verses as to what it means to live and work as a skin encapsulated ego by yourself in our competitive ME society.

THROUGH GREATER IMAGINATION

Through greater imagination there comes awareness that there is an evolving pervading fundamental consciousness, connection and oneness filling the universe. Through greater imagination we can perceive a connection, relationship and interdependence between all life. In other words, through greater imagination we can evolve a new perception of reality, life, self and society. Through greater imagination we can understand the conditions that created people who appear different than us. Through greater imagination we can have compassion and empathy for those who are traumatized, angry, hateful or competitive with us as well as like or love us. Through greater imagination we can find creative solutions. Through greater imagination we can find ways to connect, collaborate, cooperate and co-create greater complexity and love. Through greater imagination we can understand that we all come from one family of humanity, and one Gaia global biosphere of life. Through greater imagination we can liberate our skin-encapsulated egos and embrace a revolution in consciousness, a revolution in values, a revolution in our understanding of evolution, love, life, self and society. Through greater imagination we can.

EVOLVE LOVE FOR A NEW PERSPECTIVE OF THE WORLD

Let us evolve love for the world as a living-breathing planet, which I call Gaia. Let us be citizens of one country named Gaia. To do this humanity will need to evolve a friendly perspective of others, life and Gaia. We are all members of the tribe of all life on earth. Let us unite the personal and the planetary and become citizens of one interdependent living planet. Let us awaken to the fact that all of humanity is woven into Gaia as cosmic terrestrial inter-beings.

A GAIA LOVE MEDITATION

Imagine that your breath is your close friend, family member or lover, and your close friend is named Gaia. As you inhale, open your arms wide and welcome Gaia into your body temple as you would welcome a close friend, family member or lover into your home. As you exhale, bring your palms together and wish Gaia well as you would wish a friend, parent or lover well as 'te' departs. Life, Gaia, is breathing you, as you are breathing Gaia.

Inhale, open your arms wide and welcome Gaia into your body..
Bring your palms together and wish Gaia well as you exhale.

Repeat seven times.

Life is breathing you as you are breathing life.

A STORY WHICH MUST BE TOLD, YET NO ONE WANTS TO HEAR

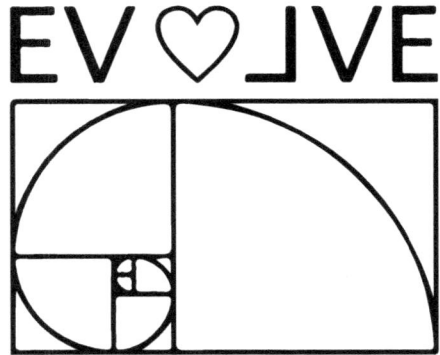

Daily evidence suggests that earth has already entered its sixth greatest period of mass extinction, not just a period of global warming. According to a Yale study, everyday 150-200 species go extinct in developed, damaged or polluted ecosystems, marshes, lakes or mountaintops. That is to say, an entire species of insects, birds, fish, plants or reptiles go extinct every 20 minutes, and are never coming back. The growth of modern human agriculture, industrialization, transportation and population has touched everyone and every species on earth. Through deforestation, mining, factory farming, herbicides, pesticides, plastics, nuclear waste and fossil fuel pollution, humanity now has disrupted, polluted or destroyed, the dynamic balance of every ecosystem on earth. Humanity and the modern world are at a tipping point between human extinction and a great new story of what it means to be human and be reunited with nature, Mother Earth, Gaia.

Humanity's presence, changes and effects on the earth are now as powerful as any asteroid; volcanic or tectonic plate movement, which resulted in past periods of mass extinction. As a result, we have entered what geologists now call the Anthropocene Epoch. The Anthropocene Epoch is described as the geological period where human activity has a substantial influence on the planet. The crises of global warming and mass extinction cannot be fixed by simply changing our technologies without changing our consciousness. It is an illusion to believe that natural gas, solar or wind energy will save us from mass extinction or global warming, without first changing our disconnected modern consumer lifestyle and consciousness. Humanity's philosophy of materialism and separation, with its disconnected selfish drive for greater property and profit is responsible for destroying the biosphere. It is humanity, not carbon, which is destroying the planet and leading to this period of global warming and mass extinction.

Our modern plantation capitalist economy, with its cosmology of materialism, separation, exploitation and competition, is incompatible with a peaceful, just, healthy and ecological world. Humanity's desire for material progress, an ever-expanding use, extraction and domination of nature for its resources, is killing the biosphere. Over 40% of all biology on earth, more than 40% of all animals, birds, fish, reptiles and insects, have died off in the last fifty years.

It seems as if humanity no longer enjoys living a life in harmony with nature, or each other. Humanity has been competing and extracting from the earth, it has already covered the globe with conflict, war, trash and pollution, while having fished out over 90% of the world's sharks, tuna, cod and swordfish. Humanity's survival of this period of climate change and mass extinction will require a sea change in humanity's values, thoughts and beliefs about what is human progress. Humanity needs to envision what it means to live an interdependent life in harmony with others and Gaia in a regenerative sustainable world.

When we support and recognize the connectivity and inter-dependency between all creatures, we begin to break free from the matrix of separation and embrace a sense of oneness.

The intersection of the explosive growth of human population, deforestation and massive wealth inequality has pushed humans and animals together in novel, strained, and toxic relationships creating environmental stress resulting in the adaptation and evolution of new and different viruses to cope with the changed environment. It could be argued that COVID-19 is a zoological virus that is the direct result of a strained, toxic and polluted intersection between humanity, poverty and the environment. Consider that COVID-19 is connected to global warming and related to this period of mass extinction.

We will all experience the traumas of this period of climate catastrophes and the toxicity of the modern world. All of humanity will be affected and ultimately will have to adapt in order to survive. Wildfires, air pollution, super storms, flooding, record droughts and toxic chemicals are challenging all of life on Mother Earth. On top of that, for so many people there is no escape from the fear, violence and death of the wars, ethnic cleansing, religious bigotry and sexism of nations. There will be no escaping from the desperation produced by the poverty, hunger and sickness of refugees from massive wealth inequality, wars and climate catastrophes. The overall health and well being of modern developed countries has also fallen with the rise of fossil fuel pollution, herbicides, pesticides, processed foods, micro plastics, electromagnetic radiation and loneliness. The rates of asthma, autism, cancer, suicide, infertility, diabetes, obesity, drug addiction and autoimmune disorders have all skyrocketed in our modern world. All of humanity will be displaced in one form or another. We will all be affected by a world of toxic pollution and global warming.

The story that must be told, yet no one wants to hear, is that our modern story of materialism and its soulless matrix of separation are not only making us sick, they are killing us and the rest of the planet. Humanity now has the ability to care for, feed, clothe and shelter the world's people. However, humanity has not evolved the love to do it.

Humanity also has the knowledge and capacity to stop polluting and destroying the biosphere, however humanity does not have the heart to do it. Nevertheless, humanity does have the capacity to change, evolve and do it. Humanity can evolve greater connectivity, coherence and consciousness with nature. In other words humanity can evolve a cosmic inter-being love and adapt a new understanding and perspective of interdependence and co-create, regenerate and resonate with the biosphere. Let us save all the ecosystems, plants, animals and life we can. Let us understand that there is enough for humanity's need but not for humanity's greed.

IMAGINE A NEW STORY OF LIFE AND EVOLUTION

In this moment of mass extinction, we can imagine that the earth, Gaia, is now headed into a new age of transformation and evolution. Let us awaken to the fact that according to the fossil evidence, evolution takes place in leaps, not gradual steps like so many of us were taught in school. In other words, Darwin's concept that evolution takes place slowly and gradually over time has not been borne out by the fossil record. After hundreds of years of excavation, paleontologists have not found intermediate species to support the notion of incremental evolution. All of the fossil records indicate that evolution takes place in a qualitative leap, not in gradual incremental steps. Think of how past periods of massive climate change radically transformed the biosphere creating a new and different environment setting the stage for new viruses and species to adapt and evolve, for a leap in evolution. It seems that evolution is not so much about the survival of the fittest, especially in the modern sense of fitness as simply about an individual's physical fitness.

Evolution is about viruses, bacteria, plants and animals ability to transform, adapt and evolve together to a changed environment. Could it be that cooperation between species and symbiotic inter-nested relationships rather than competition and individual fitness, is what is critical for evolution. Imagine that the world is a friendly place and that evolution is based upon cooperation between individuals and between species instead of competition. Could it be that evolution might be based upon the survival of the friendliest as opposed to the fittest?

To save the biosphere for the human species, and the majority of the worlds species' survival in this new era of climate change and mass extinction will require humanity to dream of, believe in and revel in an outrageous love of inter-being and inter-nested life. It is time for an outrageous unconditional love of life that leads us to dance with each other and the tribe of all life on earth. To evolve an outrageous love of life is to transform our perception of separate life forms and awaken to the truth that all life is inter-nested and interdependent. Humanity is killing itself with its story of materialism and separation, which have created modern global capitalism, pollution, war and toxic unsustainable growth. It is time to evolve a new story of life. It is time for a radical outrageous love of life, which compels us to change and transform ourselves in order to save the biosphere and ourselves from ecocide.

To adapt a story of a cosmology of oneness is to evolve a sense of inter-being, a friendly feeling of connection and compassion for others beyond our immediate family and species. It is to recognize that we need each other, and that we all need to feel love, be loved and witness love.

Let us feel this moment in our bones, hearts and DNA to change and take a transformational leap of consciousness into an outrageous unconditional love of self, others and life. Let us feel and embody a common sense of purpose and solidarity with all of humanity and all of life on Gaia. It is time to collaborate, resonate and take action together to evolve a new sense of interdependence, self and world where we can work, play and co-evolve together in a healthy sustainable manner.

To heal the biosphere for humanity's survival, the human species, Homo sapiens, will need to take an evolutionary leap in consciousness, a leap from separation to unification, from a disembodied spiritual connection to each other and Gaia, to an embodied spiritual connection and love for each other. It is time for Homo sapiens to wake up, adapt and evolve to a changed environment of global warming and mass extinction. In order to save humanity from itself, it is time for, humanity to dream and awaken to a sixth sense perception of inter-being consciousness and connection and break free from the matrix of separation. It is time for humanity to embody spirituality, a love spirit consciousness to collaborate, share and resonate together with one cosmic inter-being consciousness and love to co-create a new sense of being in a WE-ME Society and world.

EXPAND YOUR HEART CAVITY AND TAKE A LEAP IN CONSCIOUSNESS

Inhale to your solar plexus, your navel center, your sense of self, and let it lift your heart. Stimulate the flow of the blood and breath in your chest through circular, robust, rhythmic breathing. Increase the flow of your breath with the vigorous inhalations and forceful exhalations of equal length. Pretend your forearms are handles on an accordion or a bellows. As you inhale lift and open your forearms, the handles of your imaginary accordion or bellows, exhale and close them. Inhale and lift and expand the heart cavity. Increase the rhythmic flow of the breath as you vigorously inhale and lift the heart forward, raise the shoulders and then exhale smoothly and forcefully as you close your arms. Increase the flow of energy around, in and through your heart's vortex field. Start slowly. Have a tissue handy.

Vigorous breathing loosens phlegm and mucus. Note: It might be easier and more beneficial to exhale through your mouth and inhale through your nose. Practice both ways.

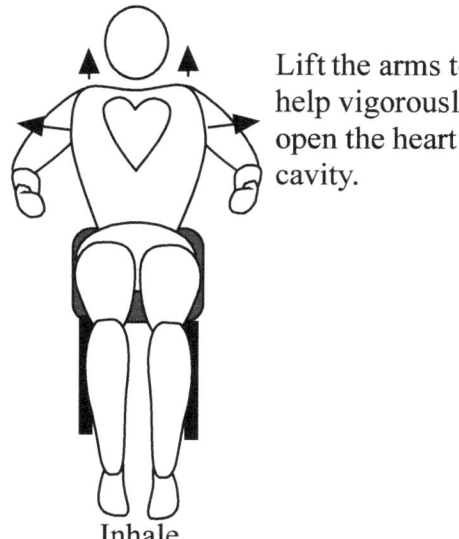

Lift the arms to help vigorously open the heart cavity.

Inhale

Inhale Vigorously

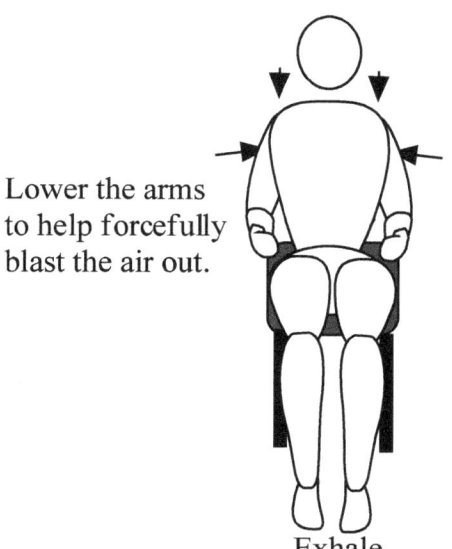

Lower the arms to help forcefully blast the air out.

Exhale

Exhale Forcibly

Inhale vigorously and exhale forcibly 10 times.

Pause, move into stillness and close your eyes.

Experience a sense of cosmic oneness and evolve love..

Change your perspective, view and thought of what it means to be human and experience reverence and compassion for the connectivity and interdependence of all life. Imagine humanity's and your metamorphosis and evolve a sense of inter-being, of humano unam for the health and well being of yourself, others and the planet.

DREAM OF AND IMAGINE YOUR INTER-BEING CORE OF ONENESS

Modern concepts of our core are physical in nature and exclude any spiritual or paranormal wonders of human beings. Modern science and culture have typically described our core as the physical muscle groups deep within the abdomen and back that attach to the spine and pelvis. However, long before the expressions core strength, core power and core workout became popular, spiritual traditions wrote about our core differently. They have often referred to our core as a core of goodness. Connecting to your core of goodness is to experience your cosmic love spirit consciousness as, immortal and true, as a localized expression of cosmic inter-being consciousness.

Think of the image of an apple core when thinking about the core of the human body. An apple core goes from the stem through the entire apple. When we activate our core, we align a field of energy that radiates out through our entire body. This field of being is a subtle vortex field that is sustained by the electromagnetic energy of each heartbeat, thought and the subtle spiritual energy of each breath.

The word core is a late 14th century English word likely derives from Old French, coeur, and meaning : heart. Your heart is at the center of your core. Your heart is your single largest source of electro-magnetic energy of your body, even more than your brain. The belief that the heart is merely muscle that serves as a mechanical pump is antiquated. The heart is more like an electromagnetic vortex mixing and regulating our blood flow. The heart produces hormones to help regulate our metabolism and serves like a body-brain that communicates with the brain, body and gut through pulse waves, hormones, the nervous system and electromagnetic fields. The subtle energetic field generated by our hearts creates a dynamic toroidal donut shaped whirlpool vortex around us. Toroidal whirlpool vortex fields are the sacred archetypal form for all self-organizing structures. Red blood cells, trees, galaxies and people all create their own unique whirlpool vortex field of energy.

In the yoga tradition, our core is often referred to as our kundalini or pure consciousness. Imagine that your core is not physical at all, but rather a unique cosmic vibrating whirlpool field of consciousness centered in your heart. Connecting to our 'core' is connecting to the locus of consciousness, the unique cosmic tone, the vortex field of spirit that is us. Connecting to our core is being able to imagine and visualize that we are unique vortexes in one ever expanding cosmic sea of inter-being spirits.

Resonate and breathe with the core of your being. Let us travel with the warp speed of consciousness to co-create a new social state based on heart felt core values of compassion, coherence, love and reverence. Let us rebel against our cosmology of materialism where the world is made up of physical forces in a soulless matrix in which feelings, thoughts, beliefs and love are considered the result of physical forces. For example, the typical modern English translations of the ancient yoga word prana include life force or life-giving force. The word force is connected to materialism through the classical Newtonian physics equation, force equals mass times acceleration. An ancient quantum definition of prana might describe it not as a force but rather as a vibrant subtle inter-being spiritual life energy, connection and information.

Prana as mysterious inter-being life energy information has been recognized by ancient cultures around the world. *Prana* has been equated to the Chinese *chi,* Japanese *ki,* Polynesian *mana,* Native American *orenda,* African *ashe* and the ancient German *od.* Some scholars say that the modern English word God comes from the ancient German word *od.* In a cosmology of oneness, there is one cosmic inter-being consciousness which animates, sustains and loves all life.

OPEN YOUR 6ᵀᴴ SENSE OF PERCEPTION

YOUR CORE CONNECTION TO A COSMOLOGY OF INTER-BEING ONENESS TUNE INTO YOUR 3ᴿᴰ EYE & 3ᴿᴰ EAR

YOUR COSMIC WI-FI ANTENNA

Humanity has created language, culture and technology creating a global economy, supply chain and Internet. Let us now imagine and perceive a global consciousness, a global brain, a spiritual Wi-Fi connection, a cosmic outer net. We are all familiar with our five material senses of smell, taste, sight, touch, and hearing. They provide the foundation of empirical science, yet just because you cannot empirically measure something does not mean that it does not exist, is real or valuable. In the yoga tradition, the five material senses are connected to the first 5 chakras, and our 6ᵗʰ sense is connected to our sixth chakra the invisible world of telepathy, intuition and cosmic inter-being communication.

The 6th chakra, Ajna Chakra is where the ida and pingula nadis, yoga channels of subtle energy in the body, come together for an understanding of our self and reality beyond our five senses. Chakras are psychophysical vortex centers, which are associated with different physical senses and glands in our endocrine system. The pituitary and pineal glands are associated with our 6th chakra. Even though we typically only think of the 6th chakra as our 3rd Eye, at the brow point, there is a flip side to our 6th chakra, our 3rd Ear. Connecting to the Ultimate Reality beyond our five material senses is about connecting and creating coherence between the 3rd Eye and the 3rd Ear, a paranormal sense of a cosmic Wi-Fi connection.

THE YAWN REFLEX

Begin opening your 3rd Eye and 3rd Ear, through yawning. The yawn reflex stimulates the eyes, ears, and a parasympathetic relaxation response in the body and mind. Yawning stimulates the eyes to tear. It has been suggested that animals in the wild yawn before they go to sleep to open their ears to any strange sound as they sleep. A good strong yawn reflects suspends your sight and hearing for a moment, so your eyes can tear, and your ears can pop. Yawning is like rebooting your brain. Yawning as a great way to release any mental patterns of tension and anxiety. Stimulate the yawn reflex, clear your thoughts and open your eyes and ears to a cosmology of oneness.

Lie down, lift your hips and slide a block, cushion or folded blanket under your hips. Relax the front of the body. Open your heart. If the low back is pinching, try tightening the buttocks for a moment or lowering the height of the blankets. Take the arms overhead and create a yawn stretch.

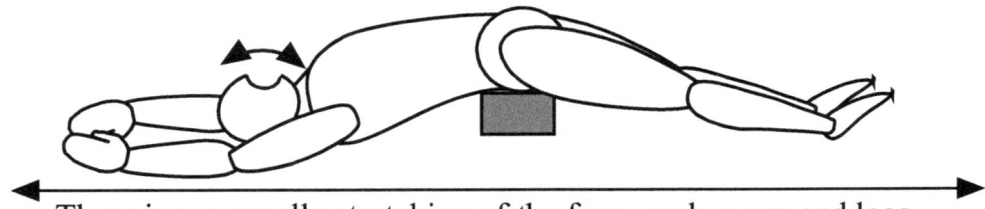

Inhale

The palate rises into the brain cavity and there is a tendency to move the tongue downward and to the rear of the mouth as the jaw opens wide.

There is a generally stretching of the face, neck, arms and legs.

Press the back of the head into the floor as you look to the wall behind you; cool the roof of your mouth as you inhale the sound of 'aaa' as you create the yawn reflex. Practice until your eyes begin to tear opening your 3rd Eye. Open your mouth wide as you yawn and let your ears pop. Release your feelings of anxiety, stress and separation, and open a sixth sense of perception, oneness and a feeling of total acceptance in a cosmic sea of oneness.

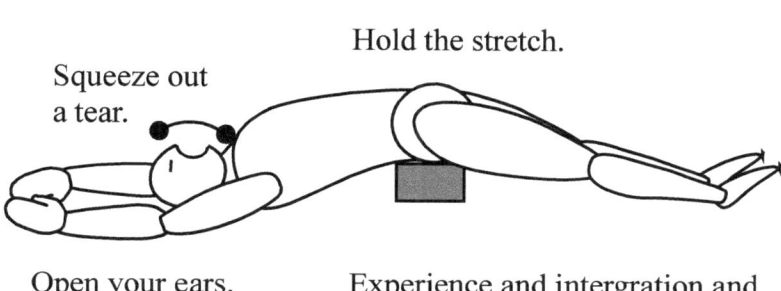

Exhale

Hold the stretch.

Squeeze out
a tear.

Open your ears.

Experience and intergration and
a new awareness.

EEG

Electroencephalography (EEG) is the recording of electrical activity along the scalp. EEG measures voltage fluctuations resulting from ionic current flows within the neurons of the brain. The EEG electrodes are positioned on the International 10-20 System of conventionally defined locations. These locations are based on first establishing the position of the inion and then the nasion, and half way between them is the vertex.

Visualize how the pituitary gland is behind the nasion or the brow point, and that the pineal gland is in front of the inion, the protrusion on the occipital ridge of the back of the head. It could be that the joining of the cosmic essences of the pituitary and pineal glands, our 3rd Eye at the nasion, and our 3rd Ear at the inion, opens our 6th sense of perception, telepathy and our ability to resonate and connect with all life forms on a cosmic paranormal inter-being connection.

The vertex is the half way point between the nasion and the inion at the top of the head.

The inion is the prominent bump on the occiptal bone at the back of the skull.

The nasion is the depressed area just above the bridge of the nose.

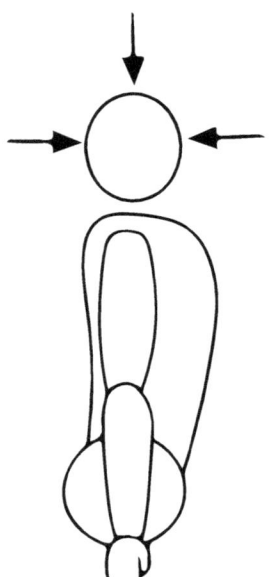

Scientists in the 20th century did not have the technical abilities to do in-depth research on the brain yet often asserted that humans used only 10% of our brains. New studies are continually being released and it is not difficult to imagine that part of the other 90% of our brains are for unknown paranormal abilities like a 6th Sense, a cosmic telepathic ability to sense, communicate and resonate with others and all life including the inter-nested life of our gut biome. Imagine that yoga postures are like templates to resonate and communicate with nature, plants, animals and insects. Imagine that through conscious breathing and posture one could connect to a cosmic connection beyond our five senses. Let us tune into, resonate and communicate intentions, thoughts and feelings of others. Imagine that inhalations create nerve impulses to the brain receiving a cosmic telepathic cosmic Wi-Fi signal. Imagine that exhalations create nerve impulses from the brain radiating a signal and sending a message, thought, feeling or intention through your 3rd Eye.

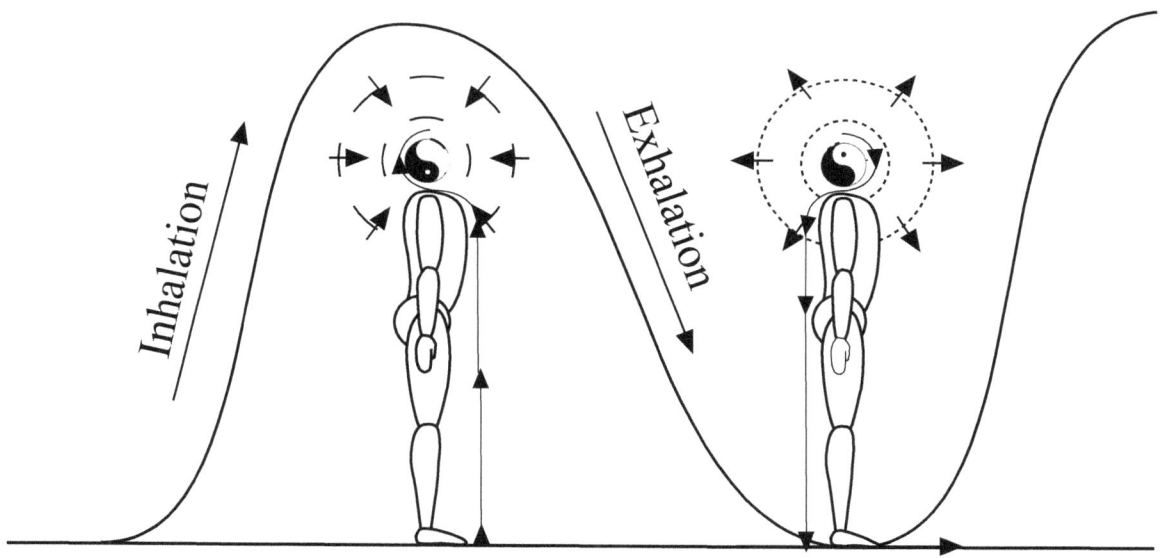

Inhale to the inion, open a core connection, a cosmic inter-being Wi-Fi connection and tune into intuition, subtle messages, insights, intelligence and premonitions. Exhale out of the nazion and send out subtle cosmic Wi-Fi transmissions of intentions, love and wisdom. Practice breathing into this deep connection and experience a dynamic paranormal connection of cosmic oneness. Listen to and resonate with the vibrant ocean of life on Gaia and experience Gaia's love for you.

Turn on your cosmic antenna. To help establish a cosmic Wi-Fi connection you could have an altar. An altar is a portal to the invisible cosmic Wi-Fi space of one love spirit consciousness. An altar, be it as small as a seed in your pocket or as big as the ocean, becomes a metaphysical doorway to connect to a cosmic oneness.

Inhale into the inion, and listen for an inter-being cosmic Wi-Fi transmission.

Exhale out of the nasion, and transmit an inter-being cosmic Wi-Fi message.

THE DAWNING OF A NEW AGE

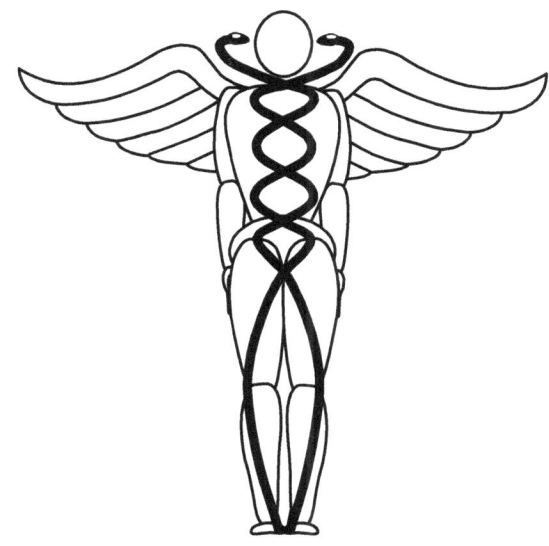

In many respects humanity is at the dawning of a whole new cosmic age of understanding spirituality, reality, life and nature, not just the end of the modern era. For thousands of years humanity has had a cosmology of materialism, a binary polarized spirituality, in which the physical was separated from the spiritual, matter from space, humanity from nature and men from women. Women have been objectified, oppressed, abused and treated as inferior for thousands of years in both religion and society. During this past age humanity's major spiritual traditions, Christianity, Judaism, Islam, Hinduism, and even the practice of yoga, adopted a toxic patriarchal spirituality and society. Religions adapted a binary polarized approach to spirituality, in which spirit and consciousness were separate from the physical body, women and nature. During this past age of spirituality heaven was separated from earthly life. In the classical yoga tradition of Patanjali, purusha, the soul or consciousness, was separated from prakriti, all physical material and the natural world. The body, and its recently discovered gut biome, was separate from the soul, and often was referred to as merely a food tube, or a meat sack. Spiritual seekers sought practices to achieve a transcended disembodied spirituality detached from earthly life.

Enlightenment was accomplished with inner spiritual practices, while renouncing outer personal possessions, society and women. This was the path to enlightenment of blissful pure consciousness, independent and separated from the physical world. That is to say humanity's world religions have sought a transcendent spirituality independent from earthly concerns.

For millennia men have tried to achieve spiritual enlightenment renouncing the body, society and the feminine, as obstacles to enlightenment. We are all familiar with past stories of the spiritual seeker going into a cave, monastery or to the mountaintop to meditate free from the concerns, joys and worries of society and daily life. The reason being was that earthly things were not considered spiritual, sacred or divine. The spiritual aspirant sought eternal pure consciousness independent of the temporal physical sensations, earthly life and women. Living a life in society was considered secondary, and even independent from, attaining spiritual enlightenment. The implication being that an individual could achieve enlightenment separate from relationships with others and Gaia.

In other words, for thousands of years world religions have asked men to give up their humanity in order to find their divinity.

Our modern world religions are based on a disembodied spirituality detached from the body, women and the natural world. It has separated the personal from the social, leading to the notion that one could achieve enlightenment and well-being renouncing inter-being and interdependent relationships. However, to evolve love for a sense of oneness and embody spirituality is to integrate the body, earthly life with nature and others into a living spiritual enlightenment, rather than renounce and transcend them. In other words, let us embody spirituality and co-create heaven on earth. Sri Aurabindo, the founder of Integral Yoga, who at the turn of the 20th century described the spiritual history of yoga for the last thousand years as basically one of renunciation. He described an enlightenment that did not affect those around him as having a stale taste. He advocated that all of life is spiritual, and in his words, "All of life is Yoga." The Buddhist tradition describes this non-dual philosophy of heaven on earth, as Nirvana equals Samsara.

To make one cosmic inter-being spirit consciousness a reality in this new age is to adapt a non-dual embodied spirituality and create a heaven on earth in which everyone and everything is sacred, divine and connected. Let us evolve love for an Aquarian conspiracy for greater biodiversity, connectivity and coherence in both nature and society by respecting and honoring the water cycle of Gaia. Let us celebrate life connecting social, political, economical and ecological issues in our daily life through dancing, nonviolent civil disobedience, gardening, voting, regenerative agriculture, recycling, breathing and more.

Progress, through the development of technology for greater control over our environment for humanity's benefit, has been considered a positive thing, in spite of its recent disastrous effects on the planet. For thousands of years this technological progress of society has been fueled by fires burning forests, coal, oil and gas. Progress in the age of Pisces was built on top of nature through the expansion of agriculture, destroying the forests and damming the rivers. The Age of Aquarius will be an age of co-creation and coherence with Gaia and reverence for the water and carbon cycles of life. Technological progress in the modern era has been about improving humanity's control, domination and extraction of nature. Social progress in the modern era has been about improving inclusion and equality in our social and economic political systems. In that respect progress is about reforming systemic separation, inequality and injustice. That is to say, progress is an incremental reform of the current materialist capitalist society so that it is fairer and more just, yet never creating a possibility of total equality, justice or environmental more incremental steps.

This new age of spirituality seeks to abolish the concept that the history of humanity is about the story of the deeds of great men, but rather the history of humanity is about the integrative human development of language, culture, community, social beliefs, technology and the interdependent symbiotic web of life, as the true driving forces of change. There is no need for monuments to the Dark Lords of the matrix of materialism, sexism, genocide and colonialism. Humanity has no need to glorify or horrify individuals. When it comes to criminals and mass murders, instead of looking at them as simply bad apples, or lone wolves, it is time to look at society, as a bad barrel, as a soulless matrix of separation, which is ultimately responsible for housing and ripening the bad apples of society.

This new age of spirituality represents an inter-being embodied spirituality and activism that seeks to abolish all forms of ideological and institutional control, separation and oppression. Consider that the spiritual activism that began with the movement to abolish` slavery now focuses on the abolishment of current systems of control and domination, such as jails, prisons and detention centers. This is a New Age, an age of non- dual social-spiritual movements, which connect spiritual, and social, international and environmental justice issues.

To evolve an outrageous love of life

in this new age of embodied spirituality

is not only to advocate for the abolishment of jails, prisons and detention centers,

as much as it is the abolishment of a society that <u>could</u> have them.

A WIN-WIN SOCIETY

Life on Gaia is about win-win symbiotic relationships. Ecosystems are about co-creating win-win situations between insects, plants, bacteria, fungi and animals and vice versa. Life is based on symbiotic inter-nested relationships in which all benefit in some way to evolve greater biodiversity, connectivity and coherence in the web of life. Life need not be viewed as a competition or a war between winners and losers. Life is a complex dynamic web of relationships and cannot be simply reduced to one-sided relationships where the winner takes all.

A Win-Win Society and world creates a win-win between feminine and masculine energies and between Gaia and humanity. Through an embodied spirituality grounded in reverence, friendship, and a 6th sense of perception, a cosmic Wi-Fi connection humanity can imagine, co-create and evolve a new social contract and state, a Win-Win Society. This Win-Win Society is a post-modern society uniting spirituality and science, while balancing policies of personal responsibility, morality and liberties with policies of social and planetary responsibility, morality and liberties. This win-win ideology is a 'wins-dom' philosophy where women and men, poor and rich, share in the fruits of society's wealth, infrastructure and technological development while maintaining the health and well-being of ecosystems and the biosphere. A win-win ideology is a regenerative philosophy about co-creating between men and women, nations, and ultimately between humanity and Gaia.

To create a Win-Win Society, a WE-ME society and world guided by a sense of connection and unity, humanity will need a cosmic inter-being spirituality, which embraces women and all of life. To embody an outrageous spirituality is to expand the connectivity and coherence between seemingly separate individuals, life forms and social issues. In a non-dual cosmology of oneness there is no need for a dividing or polarizing approach to people, nature or social issues. Everything is connected, everything is sacred.

Ultimately, to evolve one cosmic mind, heart and love in this new age of spirituality is to adapt an embodied grounded spirituality with an inter-being sense of self and reality where the personal meets the planetary and the local meets the global. In other words, instead of looking at individuals as separate people let us see ourselves as inter-nested holobionts, Gaians, and connected inter-beings. In order to survive this period of global warming, climate catastrophes and ecocide, humanity urgently needs to break from the soulless modern world of materialism and separation.

It is time to transform the dominant culture, the barrel, the social contracts and institutions in which we live. There is a primordial fundamental love spirit consciousness in all of us, and all phenomena. Let us perceive an outrageous spirituality of oneness, one love, one planet of inter-being spirits. Let us evolve a radical vibrant spirituality and consciousness to integrate and re-generate humanity and the biosphere. Rebel against the matrix of materialism and separation that divides us. Evolve love for a cosmology of oneness, and a 6th sense of perception, connection and love of Gaia and each other. Revel in one beautiful Gaia love story and evolve a new perspective of evolution, love and life.

Become a Gaian global villager, a Cosmic Dancer, a world citizen and co-create a WE-ME Win-Win Society and heal you, others and the planet.

EQUAL RATIO BREATHING

Let us balance and integrate the feminine and masculine qualities of our breath, being and society. Let us activate our feminine yin in-breaths and relax our masculine yang out-breaths. May our breath and spirits be united in a rhythmic circular manner like the yin and yang symbol smoothly moving up, around and down, like wings in flight.

Equal ratio breathing is a great way to slow and balance the breath by inhaling for the count of five seconds into a brief pause, and then exhale to the count of five seconds into a brief pause. Practice seven times.

THE GAIA REV♡LUTION

A WE-ME WIN-WIN REVOLUTION
A GAIA LOVE REVOLUTION

A Gaia Love Revolution in this new age of embodied spirituality, is about humanity awakening to a cosmology of oneness and a 6th sense of connection to co-create a Win-Win WE-ME society, philosophy, morality and world. A Gaia Love Revolution is about humanity's evolution and understanding of love and life. It is a leap into a cosmology of oneness which perceives one cosmic inter-being animating all of life. We are all entangled. Humanity is connected with one cosmic mind, one biosphere, one water cycle of life and one carbon cycle of life. Let us be connected with a sixth sense, a cosmic Wi-Fi connection through a radical cosmic love spirit consciousness.

A Gaia Love Revolution is based on a holistic integrative, interdependent and inter-being sense of self, others and the planet. The notion that we can, or will heal our bodies and physical constitution, or our economy and legal constitution without addressing our physical and spiritual relationships with Gaia, and the rest of humanity, is impossible.

A GAIA LOVE REVOLUTIONARY PHILOSOPHY OF LIFE, LIBERTY AND THE PURSUIT OF HAPPINESS

Modern capitalist society's notions of life, liberty and the pursuit of happiness were founded in a soulless matrix of materialism and separation and the notion that people, and nations, primarily function as encapsulated egos. It is a modern materialist myth that an individual's life, liberty and happiness could be separated from other lives or the web of life in any meaningful way. Life is a symbiotic holistic interdependent phenomenon and there is no such thing as a separate life form. We are all inter-beings part of one water cycle of life in one living biosphere. To guarantee someone life is to guarantee him, her or 'ter' air, water, shelter, community and a biosphere to live in that are not polluted and toxic. It is only through a belief in materialism and separation could one conceive of a life physically, mentally and emotionally separated and disconnected from other lives. Remember that you are not even a single life form, but rather you are composed of trillions of mitochondria living in every cell of your body, and a gut biome of bacteria, fungi and protozoa all of which have their own DNA. It is amazing to consider that all of these little microscopic creatures make up 90% of your body mass. All life is inter-nested and woven together. Your gut feelings are literally the needs and feelings of billions of bacteria and fungi calling out to you. It is time to include ecology, biodiversity and a sense of inter-nesting and inter-being in our health, relationships and contracts.

Our modern concepts of life, liberty and the pursuit of happiness were considered in the context of materialism, sexism, aristocracy and colonialism. In the beginning of the European modern era legislative rights of liberty were reserved only for property owning white men. In fact, it's important to remember that the original words in the first draft of America's declaration of independence read, life, liberty and the pursuit of property.

A Gaia, Mother Earth, concept of liberty will be based on the dynamic relationships between the needs and liberty of the individual and the needs and liberty of others in the web of life. However, this can only take place if the individual perceives "terself" as connected with Gaia. In other words, someone's individual rights, freedom and needs must be understood in the context of the rights, freedom and needs of Gaia and other human beings.

Modern science and society have created a cosmology of soulless matter, private property and a dead mechanical universe where your life can be considered as a discrete separate life. As a result, the concepts of modern liberty are considered in the context of a separate individual being. A Gaia post-modern concept of liberty needs to include the concepts of interdependence, symbiosis and ultimately a sense of inter-being. Once we recognize how all of life is connected, we can no longer have life, liberty and happiness for one life without considering the life, liberty and happiness of other life. In this Gaia Love Revolution, in this age of Aquarius, let us understand that," water is life" and that there is an urgent need to honor and respect the water cycle of life on earth and heal our lakes, rivers, aquifers, marshes and oceans. Consider that we will have to have a healthy blue planet before we will have a healthy green planet.

A Gaia post-modern concept of owning land will go beyond simply granting property rights to owning land without regards to the air, water, and life on the land. A Gaia inter-being view of liberty considers the rights of other people to live and grow, as well as the rights of the soil, plants and ecosystems to live and grow. In a cosmology of oneness, we are one with each other and one with the land, Gaia. In a deep ecological understanding of interconnectedness, we are the land, and need to respect and honor the land and the carbon cycle of life through organic, sustainable and regenerative forest farm gardens.

An inter-dependent and inter-being sense of self changes our conception of pursuing happiness. Happiness, a modern concept of pursuing happiness has been based upon the notion that an individual can be happy through owning property, pursuing material objects and individual wealth. A Gaia inter-being concept of wealth is based on the health and well-being of biodiversity and ecosystems in the web of life. Modern thought tends to think of happiness as only a personal experience, as if other people and nature experience no compassion, sadness or connection with us. A post-modern concept of happiness cannot be based upon the happiness of skin-encapsulated egos pursuing private gain, but rather on the pursuit of happiness of inter-dependent beings pursuing a sense of WE-ME Win-Win well-being.

The crises of today call for a Gaia Love Revolution with a new philosophy of life. Humanity needs to evolve love for a healthy planet and biosphere in order to have any meaningful and sustainable sense of life, liberty and happiness. It is time for an interdependent and inter- being approach to people, countries and nature. Humanity needs to include Mother Earth, Gaia, in its social contracts, political parties and structural institutions.
It is time for an 'earth democracy' which acknowledges and honors the rights of animals, plants and eco-systems to live and grow. It is time for humanity to become a steward of the land, soil, plants, animals and water. It is time for humanity to shepherd biodiversity and co- create with the tribe of all life on earth.

A GAIA LOVE REVOLUTION
PHILOSOPHY CALLED CORISM

The Latin word for heart is cormeum. Both capitalism and socialism were conceived in our modern cosmology of materialism, and let us consider a new post-modern ideology and philosophy, which is conceived of in our hearts called 'corism'. Imagine that this 'corism' is grounded in heart felt spiritual values and connections to life and Gaia through reverence, compassion and a sense of inter-being. Imagine "corism" as the ideology and philosophy of a Gaia Love Revolution, which you feel, and experience in your heart, gut biome and spirit. Imagine 'corism' is a social philosophy based on a cosmology of consciousness and oneness, which would place relationships before things, people before profits, and loving life before not fearing death.

I invite you to imagine this ideology of corism; is beyond modern capitalism or socialism. Both modern capitalism and socialism were conceptualized in a cosmology of materialism and a soulless matrix of separation. Both capitalism and socialism focus on the economic means of material extraction, production and distribution in society with no sense of connection to Gaia. However, 'corism' is a philosophy about the means of perception and connection to our sacred living planet, not just the physical means of material extraction, production and distribution. Corism is an emerging philosophy of sacred economics, a heartfelt philosophy of earth democracy, a collective altruism and a radical egalitarianism with reverence for all life on earth. 'Corism' is a philosophy based on informing and connecting people together and people with nature with interdependent and inter-being heart felt spiritual connections and values.

The word capitalism comes from the Latin word for head, caput. Capitalism is based on a rationalized, utilitarian and instrumental cosmology of materialism and separation from nature. The entire concept of capitalism is based on the use of money, capital, as a medium of individual competition and production in society. Capitalist money, coins and bills, visualizes and reinforces a notion of an individualistic economy by putting a picture of an individual head of state on each of them. Capitalism is a headstrong belief in materialism where money and property come before people and the biosphere. However, we all know in our hearts, at our core, that a more sharing and caring world, a more egalitarian and beautiful world is possible.

IMAGINE THAT YOU ARE
A COSMIC ANCIENT QUANTUM INTER-BEING

In a cosmology of cosmic inter-being consciousness you are a sacred, divine beautiful localized vortex of consciousness, a co-creator of all life on earth, not simply an employer or an employee, a parent or a child. At your core you are a cosmic inter-being consciousness animated by the divine earthly cosmic inter-being consciousness, Gaia. You are like a tornado, a dance, a whirlpool, in the stream of cosmic consciousness with all of the intelligence, power, creativity, love and wisdom of Gaia and entire the universe. Rebel against the notion that you are not enough or worthless. You are enough. You are a valuable sacred human inter-being regardless of any property, money or status attributed to you or, not attributed to you. You have intrinsic value and were borne to share, co-create and evolve with Gaia and the family of humanity. Revel in the truth that you are alive and part of a beautiful cosmic love story of inter-nested and interdependent evolution.

Imagine yourself as a cosmic tornado.

As you inhale you open to the sky, and

As you exhale you spiral down and touch the earth.

YOU ARE FLAWSOME

I invite you to believe in a cosmology of oneness and see the 'awe' of a cosmic inter-being spirit in people and life no matter how flawed they appear to be. To have a cosmology of oneness, of one mind, one heart, is to be able to see yourself and others from a different perspective, from an inter-being perspective. However, we all have only a localized and limited perspective of reality, and no one is physically, emotionally and mentally perfectly balanced, and so in those respects we could all be considered slightly flawed. Nevertheless, at our core we are all awesome inter-being spiritual beings. That is to say, that we are all both flawed and awesome. We are simply 'flawsome' beautiful spiritual beings.

Ancient spiritual traditions describe your body as not being made of merely flesh, but rather as made of cosmic flowers, diamonds or rainbow light. At our core we are awesome vibrant dancing beings of the light of one cosmic consciousness.

Exhale - Sunlight.   *Inhale - Moonlight.*

Exhale and visualize yourself as a diamond sparkling in the sunlight.

Inhale and visualize yourself as a flower glowing in the moonlight.

Repeat seven times

LET US STAND TOGETHER AS ONE GLOBAL FAMILY OF HUMANITY

Humanity has traveled the earth for thousands of years. If you were to go back seven generations to your great, great, great, great, great, grandparents you would have 128 of them, which you would share with tens of thousands of cousins. It is easy to conceive that even a person on the far side of the planet is your eighth or ninth cousin. However, humanity is disconnected from a shared sense of family, fellowship, oneness and a sense of common purpose on earth. Let us consider the theory of 6° of separation which maintains that any person on the planet can be connected to any other person on the planet with no more than five inter-mediate acquaintances. Let us begin to live together as one global family of humanity in a Gaia sphere of coherence for a Win-Win WE-ME Society and world.

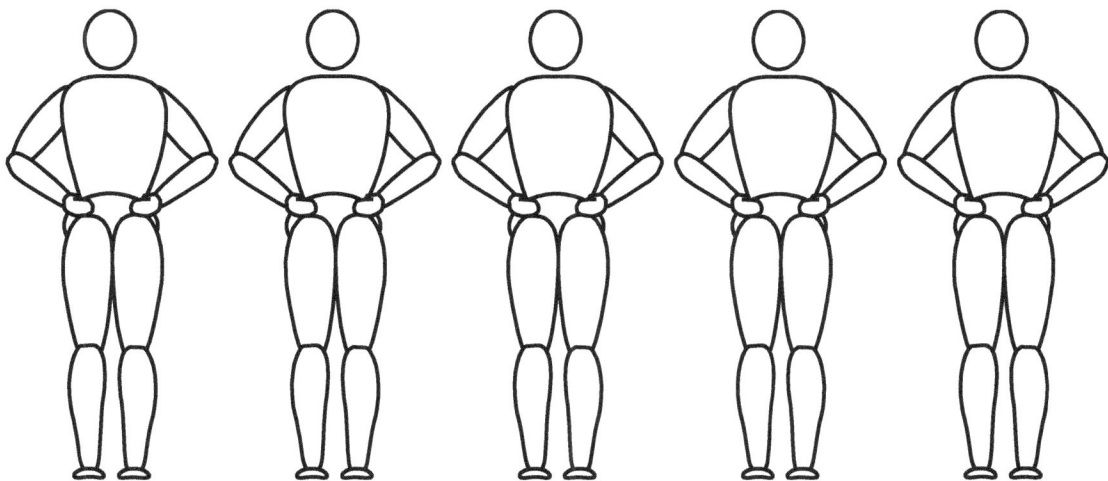

Let us stand together in fellowship and solidarity to evolve love for ourselves, each other and the web of life. Let us stand together for a sense of oneness. It is a paradox that we all must grow, learn, live and die by ourselves, yet we cannot do it alone. Let us open our hearts to a sense of inter-being and oneness. Let us stand down into peace and lower our weapons. Let us stand present beyond pride or pity and embrace one another and all life on land and sea. Let us stand together knowing that we are part of one beautiful evolving cosmic love spirit consciousness. Let us stand for a Gaia Love Revolution.

The embodied grounded spiritual state of a Gaia Love Revolutionary is a dynamic relationship between reveling and rebelling, between inner and outer, grounded and lifted, global and local, and you and I. Rebel against the matrix of separation, sexism, bigotry, war and competition between us, and revel in what unites us. To become a Gaia Revolutionary is to take the evolutionary leap into a cosmology of oneness into a world of symbiosis, connectivity, coherence, reverence and inter-being. I invite you to believe and revel in an outrageous love and an embodied spirituality, with a sense of inter-being, interdependence and entanglement between us.

EV☮LVE

EVOLVE LOVE FOR A NEW PERSPECTIVE OF PEACE

Let us evolve an outrageous love for peace. I invite you to visualize peace as a dynamic state which is connecting and balancing the polarities and complexities that create conflict between people and countries. A good peace is like a bridge, not a wall, between countries and people, just as good health is a bridge, not a wall or a bubble, between you and your relationships and the biosphere. However, it seems like ever since the "good war", World War II, warfare has become a popular model of conceptualizing and framing society's problems and issues. The modern world is full of good wars to solve its problems without any attempt to understand the complexities, which created them. America has a war on cancer, a war on terrorism, a war on drugs, a war between the sexes and a now war on COVID-19. The language of war is part of our culture and daily life as we say things like, "fight fat" or "combat stress." Let us evolve greater consciousness and let go of the desire to use the language and images of war, and killing, to frame our problems or express our desires, hopes and dreams for life. Let us evolve love for a dynamic complex peace to address our issues instead of attempting to solve our problems with war.

All wars and military actions are crimes against life and Gaia. Missiles, bombs and tanks not only damage and destroy people, communities and countries but also the biosphere of everyone else and all life on the planet through toxic air and water pollution. All wars are a form of ecocide and come at the expense of life and nuclear war threatens the destruction of all human life.

The language of war creates a culture of fear and violence with feelings of victimhood. Let us stop warring and fighting for, or against, something, someone or some nation. Let us direct our rage and anger with the whirling death machines of the modern era to evolve an outrageous love of each other and the global web of life. Let us stop fearing and fighting amongst ourselves and realize that we are all members of one family of humanity and one biosphere of life. Let us expand our compassion, connection and coherence with Gaia by imagining what it's like to walk in another's shoes, and even what it is like to be another species. Let us stop imagining that others are evil. Let us imagine the conditions in which they grew up in and realize that we would behave just like them if we had grown up in their shoes. Let us have compassion for those who are different, hateful or violent. Let us understand that it is not their fault, that it is their fault because they, in fact, were indoctrinated from birth with a cosmology of materialism and a soulless matrix of separation. It is not their fault that it is their fault that they grew up in a dysfunctional, misogynistic, racist or xenophobic family in a world of massive wealth inequality. Let us imagine that we come from the same cosmic mother and that given the same conditions we would behave exactly as them, no matter how ridiculous, awful or confusing their behavior is. Let us consider that everyone is 'flawsome'. Let us collaborate and create healing holistic inter-being relationships instead of violent competitive ones. Through greater imagination, creativity, love and wins-dom we can.

HEALTHCARE IS NOT WARFARE

We especially use the language of warfare in healthcare and medicine. To heal means to make whole; to heal does not mean to make war. Health is a dynamic balance of our whole life. In a holistic terrain theory of wellness, good health is understood as a vibrant dynamic exchange with the environment and web of life. Good health is not the absence of disease, just as a good peace is not the absence of war.

Nevertheless, the language of war and killing is regularly applied to the practice of healthcare and modern medicine. Our modern concept of medical treatment is based on the germ theory of disease in which illness is equated to a body, which is "under attack" or "besieged by invaders". Hospitals have battalions of doctors to fight and bombard the invaders. With this language and imagery of war, modern medicine creates a victim consciousness in the patient, as the patient is seen to be under attack. Rarely is the patient described as powerful or as mobilizing to repair 'terself', working to restore balance or in the process of eliminating toxins. The 'germ theory of disease' of modern allopathic medicine is based on the notion that disease is caused by pathogens from outside the patient and therefore the goal of treatment is to kill the invader. This is in contrast to a holistic 'terrain theory of wellness which considers that only in an unbalanced, toxic or damaged terrain does disease appear, and therefore the goal of treatment is to improve the terrain of the body by empowering the immune system to restore wellness and balance. Let us consciously connect to our body's natural self –healing spirit, energy and metabolic processes. Let us remember that there is more healing power in stating what you are for, than what you are against. I invite you to consider that it is only when the body and its' biome of symbiotic life forms lack an overall health and vitality do compromised metabolic and immune systems appear resulting in illness and disease.

COVID-19 has been described as an invader, and we are under attack. Let us not just fight COVID-19, let us understand viruses and their sacred role in the web of life. There are 10 to the 30 different viruses in a cup of ocean water or in a handful of healthy soil. Viruses are not living they are genetic packets of information from living bacteria and living organisms, and as a result viruses reflect changes in an organism's life or environment.

Scientists are just beginning to understand the virome and the evolutionary role viruses have played in the evolution of life on earth through horizontal gene transfer.

Let us not fear viruses and remember that exposure to germs or viruses does not always equal infection. Let us not be passive victims, but rather proactive participants in our health and immune systems. To be proactive is to be more than just being defensive, like washing our hands or wearing a mask. To be proactive means to take an active role in enhancing the vitality, health and well-being of our bodies, hearts, minds, spirits, environment and diet. As Hippocrates said, "Let food be thy medicine and medicine be thy food." Consider that 70% of our immune system is in the healthy functioning of our gut lining, our micro biome of bacteria, fungi and microorganisms. Let us be proactive spiritual beings in our health, diet, environment and relationships. I invite you to evolve love for a new dynamic peaceful symbiotic perspective of a holistic terrain theory of health and wellness in our society, institutions and treatment.

Every medical student is asked about the dangers of polarized "either or" thinking of good and bad with the question, "What is the difference between medicine and poison?" The answer requires a non-dual, a holistic understanding of health and wellness. The answer is paradoxical for nothing is simply therapeutic or toxic. Everything is sacred.

Dosage is the answer, for too much of anything is toxic. Nothing is inherently therapeutic or toxic. A weed is a plant whose virtues have yet to be discovered.

To adopt a cosmology of consciousness in our medical treatment and healthcare systems will require the dominant culture to break free from the matrix of materialism and realize that we must heal and make whole our relationships and spirits as well as our bodies and diet. Simply, healthcare based on materialism, profit and victimization is bad medicine. People need to be consciously proactive in their health, not victims. At the same time people need access to a social net of community healthcare, with entitlement to clinics and hospitals as a human right. A Win-Win WE-ME concept of medical treatment and care will be based on connectivity and coherence between the health of the individual and the health of their community, environment and planet. It will also include the health of their diet and body's biome of microorganisms. A healthy society is a peaceful dynamic balance between personal consciousness, responsibility, health and empowerment, and social and planetary responsibility, health and well-being.

EVOLVE LOVE FOR A DYNAMIC PEACE

The crises of modern warfare, nationalism, poverty, sexism, bigotry and racism are all being fueled by climate catastrophes and global warming. It is now difficult to maintain the status quo of modern life, home and country. Homeless people, poor people, asylum- seekers, displaced people due to climate change and war refugees will interact or even live next to you. Stand down into oneness, a dynamic peace, health and well-being. Imagine an inter-being spirit of friendship, coherence, common purpose, and a dynamic peaceful bridge connecting you. Inhale and lift your heart, hold your heart lifted as you exhale and feel grounded. Create a dynamic piece between inhaling and exhaling, lifted and grounded, and between you and your environment. Be mindful not to observe or judge people or countries as simply stupid, mean or flawed. Look for the twinkle of cosmic inter-being consciousness in their eyes. Embody spirituality and imagine what it might be like to be them, and the conditions that might have produced their situation and behavior. Embody one inter-being love spirit consciousness and visualize everyone's beautiful spirit. Know that everyone's inter-being spirit wants to soar on the wings of a dynamic peace and harmony no matter where they come from. Witness people, situations, life, health and death with awe, reverence and a cosmic sense of peace and oneness in your heart. Evolve love.

IN CONCLUSION

Simply put, we need to evolve love. We need to evolve love to expand our perception of life and consciousness to include a cosmic inter-being connection and sacred love of all life in order to survive our modern world of materialism, global warming and mass extinction. Humanity urgently needs to break free from the soulless matrix of materialism and evolve a 6th sense of perception and embrace a cosmology of oneness. All of humanity needs to understand, vote and rebel against governmental and corporate policies of war and ecocide. At the same time all of humanity needs to revere, revel and co-create with Gaia. Let us perceive and co-create a beautiful restorative and regenerative Win-Win WE- ME Society and world. Dirt is not inert. The earth, Gaia, is alive. The soil is worth the toil.

Become a gardener, a global villager and a lover of life. Evolve love for a Gaia Love Revolution. Co-create, resonate and connect with the web of life. Awaken your consciousness and perceive Gaia's beauty and cosmic inter-being and inter-nested love for you.

However, modern science, culture and society still generally believe in a cosmology of materialism, which is based on the concept of solid inert matter where plants, animals and people are separated by an empty space. Therefore, modern science, culture and society have considered that the act of viewing, looking, perceiving and observing someone, has no effect on them. In other words, the conscious observation of people and the natural world is assumed to be disconnected, objective and passive. That is to say, it is a modern belief, and misunderstanding, that nothing changes when you simply look at it. Modern science and society has falsely maintained that you can passively and secretly observe things, people and life without effecting or changing them in any way.

Nevertheless, how you look at and observe people, plants and animals matters. There have been numerous experiments showing the effects of observing plants with positive or negative intentions and feelings. That is to say that plants grow differently when observed by people with love and compassion as opposed to animosity and hatred. The expression, "Sticks and stones can break my bones but words can never hurt me" is a good example of how modern thinking maintains that only the physical world has any important or meaningful effect on us.

The invisible subtle fields and streams of consciousness, intentions, feelings, thoughts, beliefs and love are real and are the source of miracles in our lives. Words, thoughts and beliefs can hurt or heal. The idea that anyone, even a doctor or teacher could passively and objectively observe patients or students without affecting them, either positively or negatively, is completely false. What we believe matters when we look at and observe people, plants and animals. Doctors will no longer answer the question, 'How long do I have to live?' This is because patients tend to trust and believe in their doctors, and therefore tend to live or die into what they say. What you believe, what you hold dear in your heart, is real, and is literally a matter of life or death. Remember that the placebo, and it's polar opposite the nocebo, are real unexplainable paranormal human phenomenon, and their existence is completely statistically verifiable.

Quantum physics and ancient wisdom maintain that everything is the creation of an intelligent cosmic mind spirit consciousness. When under observation, electrons seem to be "forced" or "informed" to behave in one way or the other depending on how they are observed. Light beams behave like waves or particles depending on how you consciously choose to observe them. The act of conscious observation literally affects the outcome of experimentation, patients and students. How you look at life and people changes them.

> *"When you change the way you look at things,*
> *The things you look at change."*

To be a Gaia Love Revolutionary is to change the way you look at and perceive Gaia, people and things from one of materialism and separation to one of unity, awe, reverence and friendship in our hearts, ears and eyes. It is to witness a sense of inter-being and connection. It is to have a transformative vision which perceives a beautiful cosmic universal oneness in yourself, others and nature. In a cosmology where consciousness is primary, the popular modern saying, "I'll believe it when I see it", needs to be reversed and turned around to read, "I'll see it when I believe it." We need to believe in a friendly cosmology of oneness before we see it and can have a sense of inter-being to witness the unity and interdependence of all life. Humanity needs to believe that we are one before nations will put an end to war. People need to truly believe in equality and justice for all people, before it will happen. We need to believe we are part of Gaia and the biosphere before we will stop destroying them. We need to believe that we are loved by Gaia before we will feel that we are loved by Gaia. We have to imagine, awaken and believe in a holographic universal cosmic inter-being spirit before we can share an inter-being love.

> *A Gaia Love Revolution is not about just changing things and society as much as it is about changing what we believe about them and ourselves.*

We are at a tipping point in the history of humanity as we have entered the 6th greatest mass extinction on earth. Our entire system of modern beliefs, thought and organization are in crises and on the edge of a paradigm shift and change. Instead of believing, understanding and perceiving the world and self through the eyes of a skin- encapsulated ego in a matrix of materialism and separation, let us take an evolutionary leap into a cosmology of oneness and perceive people, society and life through the eyes of an inter-being Gaia global villager, a Cosmic Dancer, a *humano unam*. Visualize a Win-Win WE- ME Society of 'corism', of social, economic and environmental 'wins-dom'.

3 PART INHALATION FOR HOPE AND INSPIRATION

Consciously strengthen and expand your inhalation, your yin feminine energy, with a three-part inhalation to evolve a transformative vision. Begin by welcoming one full breath in as you lift and open your heart. Pause for a moment, and inhale a bit more, pause, expand and lift your heart and chest even higher, and finally inhale a third time completely filling yourself with hope and inspiration. Hold the pause, the stillness, the cosmic space that connects us. Resonate with it. Exhale and feel hopeful and inspired to evolve love for a transformative vision of yourself, others and the world.

To be a Gaia Love Revolutionary is to have a transformative vision which perceives and sees the unity, solidarity and coherence between all of us. It is to perceive one cosmic inter-being in everyone's eyes. To have a Gaia Revolutionary transformative vision is to see the awe and beauty in everything and everyone no matter how flawed they appear to be. To be a Gaia Revolutionary is to perceive life as a net of divine mutual symbiotic and interdependent beings, all unique faces of one cosmic universal inter-being oneness.

To be a Gaia Love Revolutionary is not so much about doing something differently,

As it is about believing, loving and perceiving everything differently.

EVOLVE LOVE

Evolve love for a cosmology of oneness.

Evolve love for Gaia.

Evolve love for the oceans, rivers, streams, and the water cycle of life.

Evolve love for the land, mountains and forests, and the carbon cycle of life.

Evolve love for yourself as a beautiful cosmic inter-being.

Evolve love for those who appear or seem different than you.

Evolve love for an inter-being connection, which unites all peoples, nations and species.

Evolve love for a re-generative, just and equitable society and world.

Evolve love for a dynamic balance between individual and social liberty, health, responsibility and morality.

Evolve love for a paradigm shift, a change of script, a sea change, a revolution in values in our modern consciousness, society, nations and culture.

Evolve love for a WE-ME Win-Win society, family, community and world.

Evolve love for a Gaia Love Revolution.

Neither you nor humanity will break free from the matrix of materialism and connect to the hearts and minds of others and be coherent with them, using a language of war and competition. A Gaia Love Revolution is about coming together for greater coherence in our selves, relationships, institutions and social contracts. A Gaia Love Revolution is about a win-win for all life on earth. It is about creating a win-win consciousness, a wins-dom consciousness; so that people are not fighting and competing against each other, rather that people perceive that all of humanity is on the same team. Humanity can expand the field of friendship to include a sense of inter-being and fellowship that includes everyone and all life on earth. A Gaia Love Revolution is about greater imagination, complexity and coherence in our lives, relationships, institutions and concepts. A WE-ME Win-Win Gaia Love Revolution is about creating a dynamic balance between personal responsibility and planetary responsibility, personal empowerment and social entitlement in economics, healthcare, housing, transportation and education.. A Gaia Love Revolution is about co-creating a win-win for the family of humanity, as well as the biodiversity of plants, fungi and animals. Humanity needs to open our sixth sense of perception and create a new covenant with Gaia and the tribe of all life on earth.

A WE-ME Win-Win Society and world

is not about losing something,

or even having more of what we already have had

in our modern matrix of materialism and separation.

It is about having a different perception.

It is about perceiving everything through eyes of 'wins-dom'.

To evolve love at this moment is to perceive a revolution of values, and instead of loving property and nation states, embody spirituality and love social relationships and Gaia. Evolve an outrageous cosmic love of life and stop warring and destroying the biosphere. To be a Gaia Love Revolutionary is to breathe with a heartfelt connection to the web of life. It is to experience, feel and perceive Gaia's love as greater complexity, coherence and beauty. Call for a Gaia Love Revolution and 'corism' while breathing, chanting, standing, protesting, marching, dancing, voting, eating and living with a consciousness of one inter-being love for the biosphere and one mind for global coherence. Evolve oneness, one mind, and one cosmic love for expanding consciousness in all of our relations. Take the leap and evolve a consciousness and cosmology of oneness and become a Gaia Revolutionary.

BREATHE INTO A COSMOLOGY OF ONENESS,

1. Inhale 'I am That.' Exhale 'That am I.' Inhale I am what Thou art.' Exhale Thou art what I am.' Inhale, 'I am.' Exhale, 'Am I."

2. Hum along with the universe, your friends and all of life.

3. Cover one nostril with one finger and slow your rate of inhalation up into a pause and a moment of stillness, relax and exhale. Repeat three times each side.

4. Imagine the breath is your friend and your friend is named Gaia. Inhale and welcome your friend into your heart, exhale and wish your friend well.

5. Place the thumb and forefinger of the right hand just below your collarbones and place your left thumb in your navel and your fingertips over your pubic bone. Inhale and open the front of your body. Inhale and liberate your skin- encapsulated ego, exhale and manifest your inter-being oneness.

6. Inhale into a pause, stillness and space of oneness and exhale into a pause, stillness and space of oneness.

7. Get off of your throne of separation and align your skeletal structure with the gravitational field of the earth as you breathe.

8. Clear your mind and break free from the matrix of materialism by focusing on short sharp exhalations.

9. Expand your heart cavity by inhaling vigorously and exhaling forcibly coordinating arm movements as if you were holding on to an imaginary bellows or an accordion.

10. Inhale to the inion, your 3rd ear your cosmic Wi-Fi receiver. Exhale to the nasion your 3rd eye, and your cosmic Wi-Fi transmitter.

11. Practice equal ratio breathing by breathing out for the count of 1, 2, 3, 4, 5, pause, and breathe in for the count of 1, 2, 3, 4, 5, pause and repeat.

12. Imagine yourself as force of nature, as a cosmic tornado, As you inhale you open to the sky, and As you exhale you spiral down and touch the earth.

13. Shine your light of love. Exhale sunlight. Inhale moonlight.

14. Take a deep 3-part inhalation, and leap into a cosmology of oneness.

www.ingramcontent.com/pod-product-compliance
Lightning Source LLC
Chambersburg PA
CBHW060744070526
44539CB00076B/1892